Mayday!

Tragedy at Sea

The Sinking of the
S/S Carl D. Bradley & S/S Cedarville

James L. Hopp

CARL D. BRADLEY 50TH ANNIVERSARY EDITION

Mayday! includes more than eighty-five photographs, illustrations, and maps, as well as *Author's Notes*, documenting those two fateful days of Tuesday, November 18,1958, and Friday, May 7, 1965.

The front cover art, *"Mayday! Mayday!"*, is a painting by Kenneth E. Friedrich, in honor of Earl Tulgetske, Jr., a wheelsman on the *S/S Carl D. Bradley.* On the previous page, the black & white reverse print is from the painting by Kenneth E. Friedrich.

Matt Bellmore's drawing is featured on the back cover, a beautifully color-enhanced rendition by Amy Chojnacki. Also shown is the *S/S Cedarville* proudly a-sail on the Great Lakes.

Copyright © 2008 by James L. Hopp
All Rights Reserved
Published in the United States of America by
James L. Hopp

ISBN: 978-0-9799270-5-8

~~~~~ ✸ ~~~~~

Respectfully, to the
people of Rogers City,
who speak little, but say a lot,
and lovingly, to my parents,
who always have
spoken for themselves

CONTENTS

LIST OF PHOTOGRAPHS

FOREWORD

One is tempted, even now, with a nearly irrepressible urge, to be able to record the disclaimer often witnessed at this infant stage of a book: "All characters herein described are fictitious, and any resemblance to actual persons, living or dead, is purely coincidental." But the reality still exists, and those two, long days remain, not some shocking, morbid nightmare, but a stark reminder in the emotional realm of the minds of us who remember.

Human tragedy, an inherent part of our existence, strikes like a terrible, swift sword. Rogers City, Michigan, on Lake Huron's northwestern shore, has felt the deep, soul-piercing cut of that sword through tragedies at sea. Within seven years two proud ships sank into the depths of Lake Michigan and Lake Huron. The maritime disasters claimed forty-three lives. Thirty-one of the victims were from Rogers City, which became a town on the Great Lakes with the highest percentage of fatherless children.

To be sure, the scars always will remain, but the sinking of the *Carl D. Bradley* and the *Cedarville* somehow has made this 'port of grief' stronger. Ironically, human tragedy, with its emotion-tearing suddenness, has an uncanny way of uniting its victims.

Writing this book was a personal catharsis. While it meant having to relive events that the years somehow had softened, the experience also served to strengthen and reaffirm my faith in the human condition. Yet this writing of known events is not intended to revive the shock and tears of November 18, 1958, and May 7, 1965. Nor is it offered to render historical value judgements. Rather, it is presented as a memorial to those who have sacrificed their lives at sea, and as a tribute to those who still ply the Great Lakes in long, gray ships.

S/S Carl D. Bradley **(1927- 1958)** (*Calcite Screenings*)

~~~~~ ✱ ~~~~~

THINK OF

Stepping on shore and finding it heaven!
Of taking hold of a hand and finding it God's hand,
Of breathing a new air and finding it celestial air,
Of feeling invigorated and finding it immortality,
Of passing from storm and tempest to an unknown calm,
Of waking up and finding it home!

--Author Unknown

~~~~ □ ~~~~

CHAPTER 1

"To everything there is a season and a time to every purpose under the heaven . . . "
(Ecclesiastes, 3:1)

The year is 1958. The United States of America is undergoing profound change. In January the American satellite, *Explorer I,* rises toward the heavens, signaling America's entrance into the Space Age while introducing our society to a sometimes-ambivalent era of technological complexity. In late summer the mainland Chinese begin a relentless, heavy shelling of the islands of Quemoy and Matsu. President Eisenhower posts the United States' Seventh Fleet near Taiwan to shepherd Taiwanese anti-invasion forces to offshore islands. The invasion never occurs, but there is considerable foreign criticism of America's "blatant action."

Our relations with the Soviet Union worsen with the ever-widening "missile gap," Nikita Khrushchev's endless provocative threats, and Russian superiority in a "Space Race" causing increasing discomfort and cynicism at home. And Americans are hearing reports of bloodshed and discontent from a faraway, seemingly insignificant country in Southeast Asia. Washington, D.C., our nation's tempestuous political nerve center, is becoming an increasingly busy, hectic place to live.

Several hundred miles northwest of our nation's capital, the town of Rogers City, Michigan, is aware of the continuous, complex changes engulfing humanity. Nestled in Lake Huron's northwestern shoreline, Rogers City is relatively "young" in 1958. Founded in 1871 by William E. Rogers, the city had a proud history, rich in the tradition of the lumbering and mining era. The community's predominant

Polish and German ancestry developed a firm family ethic, predicated on the fundamental worth of the individual. The town could be described as "carefully progressive," with a political philosophy that espoused conservatism.

Representing home for some 3,800 people, the community enjoyed a picturesque, natural setting that was second to none. "Rogers," a popular, shortened namesake of the town, boasted a population whose pride in the community was apparent in the simplicity and meticulousness of its surroundings. A stranger, driving down the main street for the first time, would reflect that life here somehow seemed more relaxed than in the big city.

He would see active youngsters playing in well-kept yards, as they joyfully ignored life's complicated mainstream while emulating popular heroes of the day. The stranger might observe a housewife, busily hanging pristine, white sheets on wind-blown clothes lines. Perhaps she contemplated going to town that day to purchase a three-pound bag of Eight O'clock Coffee for $1.69, then later stopping at Kotwicki's Department Store to buy a pair of $6.95 dress shoes she had promised her husband.

As his journey progressed through town, the stranger would notice briskly walking pedestrians, purposely headed for business appointments or a merchant's sale. Maybe they considered world affairs, while some might have talked enthusiastically about the country's latest movie attractions, "The Fly" or "Ambush at Cimarron Pass." Continuing to a fiercely proud business district, the driver might patronize a local establishment, where he would witness a close consumer-proprietor relationship.

Should the stranger stop at the Brooks Hotel for a cup of coffee and happen to secure the acquaintance of a local, he would learn the town was nautically oriented and dependent. He would become aware that Rogers City is a limestone town, strongly committed to religious values and the work ethic. He also would discover it is the home of long, gray ships.

Calcite harbor in Rogers City, Michigan, was the home of the Bradley fleet's self-unloading ships. One of those ships, pictured here in the "frog pond" on December 12, 1952, during winter lay-up, would become part of one of the most violent chapters in Great Lakes' history.

Top to bottom: *Calcite, W. F. White, I. L. Clymer, Carl D. Bradley, John G. Munson, B. H. Taylor* (Note the tugs in front of the *Calcite* and *W.F. White*.) (*Calcite Screenings*)

~~~ ❑ ~~~

CHAPTER 2

"a time to be born . . ."
(Ecclesiastes, 3:2)

The *Carl D. Bradley* **was one of the longest gray ships.**
Built by the American Ship Building Company at its Lorain, Ohio,
shipyard in 1927, the *Bradley's* # 797 gray, steel hull was more than
638 feet in length and boasted a 4,800-horsepower turbine generator.
With a beam of sixty-five feet, a depth of thirty-three feet, and a
seemingly endless height from the top of the pilot house to the keel,
the ship was considered a "monster," dwarfing other vessels of the
Bradley Transportation Line. It was, at the time, the longest freighter
to grace the Great Lakes.

Actually, this great limestone carrier was the second ship that
bore the name *Carl D. Bradley*. The original *Bradley* was built in
1917, but that vessel's name was changed twice. It was renamed the
John G. Munson before receiving its final title – the *Irvin L. Clymer*.

(Author's Note: The Bradley *was the first of more than sixty
lake ships to be fitted with flow control fins, designed by University
of Michigan engineers to reduce stern vibrations, allowing a
smoother sailing experience.)*

The "new" *Bradley's* namesake was Carl David Bradley, who
was born in Chicago on September 12, 1860. Mr. Bradley began his
long, distinguished career in the limestone industry when he worked
in an iron foundry. As a young man, Bradley later managed several
foundries. During the 1890s, Carl moved to New York City, where he
served as an engineer for a consulting firm.

In 1911 the Chicago native took a giant step in his career
when he was named manager of the newly formed Michigan

Limestone and Chemical Company. As a result, Bradley moved to Rogers City, Michigan, to oversee the expansion of quarrying operations as general manager. Mr. Bradley was keenly aware of the great industrial demand for limestone; consequently, he developed an organization and facility to produce it.

From left, Carl D. Bradley, his wife, Emma, Mrs. MacLean (mother of *Bradley* Captain Malcolm R. MacLean), and Fred Bradley, son of Mr. & Mrs. Carl D. Bradley, at the *Bradley's* christening in Lorain, Ohio, in 1927. (*Calcite Screenings*)

Mr. Bradley, an engineer, was instrumental in organizing a fleet of self-unloader vessels at Calcite harbor in Rogers City, which became crucial links to America's growing steel-making industries. Once, when asked why he was working to make Rogers City the best town in the world, the community leader replied, "Why, it's because I live here myself. I'm selfish. I want the best neighbors in the world!" Mr. Bradley reached the apex of his fine career when he became president of the Bradley Transportation Company in 1920.

(Author's Note: Frederick Van Ness Bradley was born in Chicago on April 12, 1898, and later moved to Rogers City. He attended local schools, graduating from Rogers City High School. Fred Bradley graduated from Cornell University, Ithaca, New York, in 1921. In 1922 he married Marcia Marie Hillidge. He worked as a salesman and purchasing agent with the Michigan Limestone and Chemical Company in Buffalo, New York. He also was a purchasing agent with the Bradley Transportation Company in Rogers City from 1924 to 1938.

In 1938, Republican Fred Bradley defeated incumbent Democrat John Luecke to be elected to the U. S. House of Representatives from Michigan's 11th District. He served in the 76th and four succeeding Congresses. He served from January 3, 1939, until his death on May 24, 1947, in New London, Connecticut, while there as a member of the Board of Visitors to the U. S. Coast Guard Academy. Mr. Bradley was chairman of the U.S. House Committee on Merchant Marine and Fisheries (80th Congress). He is interred in Rogers City's Memorial Park Cemetery. Fred Bradley was the only Rogers City resident to ever serve in the U.S. Congress. His famous father, Carl D. Bradley, died on March 19, 1928.)

After its construction was completed, the *Bradley* was launched on April 9, 1927. It was christened by a proud Mrs. Carl D. Bradley, who smashed a red, white, and blue-ribbon bottle of Calcite water over the carrier's massive hull. Following a successful launch, the ship was eager to have a new home. "Home" was to be the Port of Calcite located at Rogers City, Michigan.

(Author's Note: The Bradley's *registered port was New York; however, her true port was Calcite in Rogers City. Her color schemes consisted of a white pilot house and cabin area, gray along the hull, and a red underbelly. A battery of six motion picture cameras, under Fred Bradley's direction, made a 1000-foot movie reel of the* Bradley's *launch.)*

Launching of New Steamer Carl D. Bradley

The above scenes were taken at the launching of the new steamer Carl D. Bradley at the yard of the American Ship Building Co., Lorain, Ohio, on April 9th. (1) Mrs. Carl D. Bradley, who acted as sponsor at the launching of the new steamer; (2) The Bradley leaving the ways; (3) The Bradley as she appeared just prior to the launching; (4) A stern view showing huge rudder and propeller.

April 9, 1927 – the launching of the *Carl D. Bradley* at Lorain, Ohio. Mrs. Carl D. Bradley (upper left) christened the ship. The ship was the longest self-unloader on the Lakes until 1949, when the 678-foot *Wilfred Sykes* was launched for the Inland Steel fleet. (*Calcite Screenings*)

Indeed the first arrival of the titanic carrier at Calcite was a momentous occasion for the people of Rogers City. The story of its triumphant arrival is recalled in the August 1927 issue of *Calcite Screenings*: "At exactly eight o'clock in the morning of July 28, the new steamer *Carl D. Bradley*, latest addition to the Bradley Transportation Company fleet and just completed at the yards of the American Ship Building Company, poked her big nose around Adams Point and a short time later, was given a warm welcome at Calcite by hundreds of plant employees and people from Rogers City, who came down to the docks for a sight of the handsome, new steamer.

July 28, 1927 – a red-letter day in Rogers City's history. Plant employees and local citizens greet the *S/S Carl D. Bradley*.
(*Presque Isle County Advance*)

"Operations at the plant were suspended several hours to give employees an opportunity to witness the arrival of a new boat. Automobiles were made to park outside the fines' side of the loading slip in order to keep a clear space where the boat landed. Hundreds of flags placed on the numerous buildings, locomotives, trucks, etc., fluttered in the morning breeze, and the whole affair presented a holiday appearance.

"The new tug *Rogers City*, with the Rogers City Community Band and Mrs. Carl D. Bradley and guests on board, steamed out to meet the *Bradley* . . . escorted her into the loading slip amid the shrieking of whistles and waving of flags by spectators. Village President Rudolph Dueltgen, Sr., greeted the boat party and expressed feelingly the warm interest of the community in the Company and its welfare, and commented on the huge achievement completed in the arrival of the magnificent new ship.

"Carl D. Bradley, president, responded in his usual hearty manner on the part of the organization. Justly proud of the ship which bears his name, Mr. Bradley told of its construction and paid tribute to its qualities, not failing to give credit to her officers and crew and to the men who have built her. He expressed a warm appreciation of the welcome given the *Bradley* by plant employees and the people of Rogers City.

'The new steamer *Bradley* is the longest freighter on the Great Lakes and is the largest of numerous unloader types of boats which have been built in recent years for the stone trade. The boat is six-hundred-thirty-eight feet nine inches long and has a beam of sixty-five feet, (is) thirty-three feet in depth, and is seventy-seven feet from the top of the pilot house to the keel. The unloading boom over which the stone travels is one hundred sixty feet in length. Modern aids to navigation are also part of her equipment; the gyro compass, the gyro pilot (Metal Mike) radio direction finders and similar equipment make the *Bradley* the last word in freighter construction.'"

Such a proud, joyous occasion indicated the *Bradley* was very special to those who attended its "homecoming." The monster ship, a triumph of modern marine technology, had quite a task in front of it —— loading and transporting unprecedented volumes of limestone to distant Great Lakes' ports. It did not take the giant carrier long to establish itself as a "super carrier." The mammoth steamer transported nearly fifteen thousand tons of limestone to

Buffington, Indiana, on its maiden voyage.

Some two years after it was launched, the long-deck carrier set a record for carrying the largest, single cargo ever on the Great Lakes (18,114 tons of Calcite limestone). The record endured many years, finally being eclipsed on September 9, 1952, when larger freighters were plying the Great Lakes. To appreciate the size of the record cargo in its huge hull, consider this: the heavy load would require three complete freight trains fitted with a string of one hundred railroad cars! The vessel quickly became the pride of the fleet, and the great steamer was considered "virtually unsinkable."

(*Author's Note: On November 29, 1944, while clearing the dock in the basin of the Ford Rouge Plant – with assistance of a tug – the* Bradley's *bow swung over the ore dock and struck a Hulett unloader, tipping it over.*)

As a self-unloading limestone carrier, the *Bradley* represented one of many vital links to America's industrial complex. Its precious, plentiful cargo was crucial to the success of the nation's steel mills. The varied uses of Calcite limestone the ship carried in its massive hull were evidenced in the industries that depended on the valued mineral. Calcite limestone is a basic commodity used in the production of metallic iron, steel, soap, soda ash for glass, bicarbonate of soda, and cement.

Moreover, it is utilized as a construction aggregate in road building, for ready-mixed concrete, and in general construction. Finely ground, the mineral is used as agricultural limestone, as a soil sweetener, and as an ingredient in fertilizer and stock foods.

Like other ships in the fleet, the *Bradley* carried its cargo in a row of interior hoppers. When the limestone unloading process commenced, the stone would flow from gates at the bottom of the hoppers down onto conveyor belts. Two conveyors then transported the mineral to the forward end of the vessel, where a bucket elevator lifted the limestone above the main deck, onto the conveyor system of an unloading boom. The long, 160-foot boom could be swung out over the side of the carrier, making it possible to direct cargo onto storage piles or into waiting railroad cars.

A postcard of the *Carl D. Bradley* in 1927. The postcard, printed in color, proudly displayed the *Bradley's* long, gray hull and red underbelly. (*Calcite Screenings*)

Being the *Bradley* sailed the Great Lakes, it was subject to the same risks that faced many vessels during the course of a long, hard season. Great Lakes' storms can be very violent, frenzied affairs, with many shipwreck disasters serving as gruesome reminders to those who earned their living by the sea. Sailors recognized the dangers; they accepted them as occupational hazards.

As the 1958 shipping season commenced, the Bradley Transportation Line had compiled an enviable safety record unparalleled in the marine transportation industry. It set a world record when the National Safety Council lauded company ships as the "safest fleet in the world." The award was realized when company ships logged more than two million (2,228,755) injury-free man-hours from April 24, 1955, to December 31, 1957. The accord was not the product of "luck" but was the result of a safety-conscious company and its employees. Safety meetings were a ritual on company ships, where captains stressed important safety procedures while being receptive to crew suggestions.

In addition to the day-by-day efforts of crewmen to keep each ship in top operating condition, the Bradley Transportation Line worked jointly with the United States Coast Guard and the marine classification agencies, Lloyd's Register of Shipping Inspection Service and the American Bureau of Shipping, in a regular safety maintenance program. Every year the massive, complex limestone carriers were inspected to determine seaworthiness.

The Coast Guard initiated safety procedures during winter lay-up. Inspectors checked the hull, tanks and lifesaving equipment. They also set and sealed all safety valves. Boilers were scrutinized, frequently checked under pressure to ensure safety and reliability.

During the life of a sailing ship, the inspection list seemed endless: hatches, hatch clamps, tarpaulins ("tarps"), life jackets, stern bearings, ring buoys, flares, rafts, fire drills . . . Little wonder why the fleet was considered the safest in the world!

Eager to begin its thirty-first sailing season in 1958, the *Bradley* underwent the traditional Coast Guard inspection in January. It was declared "seaworthy" for the upcoming navigation season, although the inspection revealed several weakened or missing rivets in the interior wall of a ballast tank. These rivets were replaced with bolts.

The *Carl D. Bradley* unloads a cargo of limestone at the Gary plant of the Carnegie-Illinois Steel Corporation.
In the background is the *Steamer Richard V. Lindabury,* preparing to have its cargo of iron ore unloaded.
(*Calcite Screenings*)

BASIC STRUCTURE OF A SELF-UNLOADING STEAMSHIP (S/S CEDARVILLE)

SELF-UNLOADING BOOM   RADAR   PILOT HOUSE

STERN (AFT)

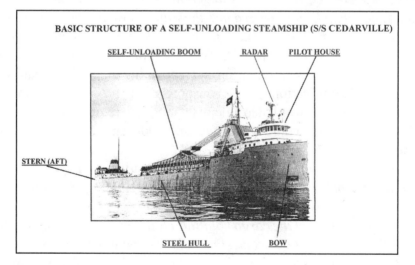

STEEL HULL   BOW

~~~ ❑ ~~~

CHAPTER 3

"a time to plant . . ."
(Ecclesiastes, 3:2)

Most of the 1958 sailing season was routine with the *Bradley* transporting over a half-million tons of Calcite limestone to distant Great Lakes' ports. The great vessel was inspected by the Coast Guard again in April, and nothing was found amiss.

(Author's Note: This inspection took place at Calcite. Commander Mark L. Hocking and Lt. Frank M. Sperry, inspectors from the OCMI Office, St.Ignace, Michigan, completed their work on April 17, 1958. A certificate of inspection was issued on that date.

On October 30, 1958, a safety inspection was conducted on the Carl D. Bradley *by Lt. Sperry. This inspection consisted of a fire drill and a boat drill, during which both boats were swung out, with the #2 life boat being lowered into the water. Twenty-eight crewmen exercised the drill, under oars, to the satisfaction of the inspector.)*

Later in the year, the Bradley Transportation Company announced its plans for repairing and renovating ships which required structural modification, a nominal procedure that was done every year. The *Bradley* was listed among those which required renovation. The huge steamer would have a new $800,000 cargo hold installed at the end of the '58 season.

(Author's Note: The work on the Bradley's *cargo hold was to be performed by the Manitowoc Shipbuilding Company in Wisconsin. It was to consist of primarily the reconstruction of the tank top, renewal of the cargo hold side slopes and screen bulkheads, and the installation of a centerline bulkhead between frames 32 and 170.)* In early November, the *Bradley* struck the lake bottom at

Cedarville, Michigan, and an inspection revealed that the grounding resulted in a 14-inch "transverse fracture" of the keel. The damage was repaired; the incident was not reported to the Coast Guard.

(*Author's Note: This fracture was repaired while the ship was afloat at Calcite by the owners' repair force. They welded a channel bar over the fracture and blanked each end to form a cofferdam. The size of this channel is not known.*)

November is an unpredictable month. Especially the weather. The thirty-five-man crew was respectfully wary of the tricky, witch-like maritime weather. But sailors also were aware the *Bradley* was a proud, faithful ship, having weathered the fiercest Great Lakes' storms for thirty-one years. The steamer's skipper, Roland O. Bryan, who lived in Loudonville, New York, was a seasoned veteran of the Great Lakes. The fifty-two-year-old Ontario, Canada, native began his long sailing career at the age of fourteen. Later Bryan spent seventeen years as mate. Then he served seven years as master before assuming command of the *Bradley* in 1954.

Ever safety-conscious, the skipper held a routine safety meeting at 6:00 p.m. on November 7. Captain Bryan stressed the importance of wearing safety equipment – hard hats, safety glasses, shoes – during the unloading of cargo.

He also cautioned crew members about dangers inherent in the fall shipping season by emphasizing the treachery of an icy deck, as well as problems created by a rolling ship in rough weather. The skipper reminded the men to keep loose material lashed down, while he encouraged them to maintain well-salted decks to avoid injury. Bryan also re-emphasized that personnel were to walk on the leeward side of the ship during periods of heavy weather.

Captain Bryan's meeting showed his concern for crew safety. He was aware of the National Safety Council's award; the *Bradley* master was determined to warrant the trust of his men. Sailors, too, recognized the importance of safety at the meeting. They suggested blowing out the deck line with air after cold-weather use. Several crewmen also warned that the deck line should never have all of the deck valves closed when de-icing was operational.

The *Carl D. Bradley* near the Mackinac Bridge.

1939 – Was the rescue ship for the crew of the stricken tug, *Badger State*

1943 – Was the first ship to go through the newly constructed MacArthur Lock (right), at the Soo

1944 – Unloading boom lengthened to 205 feet; deck strengthened

1947 – Radar system installed

(Right: *Calcite Screenings*)

A Great Lakes' sailing season is long and hard. Sailors spend most of their time on the water; hence many welcomed the arrival of November because it was the last full month seamen would spend on the Lakes. It was mid-November as the *Bradley* prepared to leave home port. The Bradley Transportation Company, a division of United States Steel Corporation, had scheduled this as the giant vessel's last trip of the year. Husbands, wives, children, and friends said their goodbyes before the ship embarked on its final lake journey of the long season. Plans for winter lay-up were in the making, with particular emphasis on replacement of the cargo hold. The forces of nature also would stamp sullen approval of the *Bradley's* "last trip."

As it left Calcite harbor for what was to be the last time, the great ship was beginning its forty-fourth trip of a long, 27,000-mile season. It was headed for Cedarville harbor to pick up a load of Dolomite limestone for delivery to Gary, Indiana. The *Bradley* exuded an image of strength and pride, as anyone can attest while observing carriers from the Lake Huron shore. Its destination, Gary, Indiana, was 411 miles from Calcite.

The trip to Gary was relatively uneventful. As the Calcite harbor melted into the water, the proud crew busily continued "routine" duties associated with running a massive lake steamer. After loading at Cedarville, Captain Bryan professionally, yet cautiously, guided the lumbering giant through the Straits of Mackinac, into the sometimes-treacherous, rock-studded northern reaches of Lake Michigan. Always wary of the dangerous Boulder Reef, the skipper carefully navigated the *Bradley* around it.

Preparing the ship for a long trek across the banana-shaped lake, Bryan reviewed his long-held respect for Lake Michigan with its vast, seemingly endless watery expanses, its unpredictable, restless, singing winds, its toiling, greenish, choppy waters.

He noted the Beaver Islands off his port bow, with the Wisconsin coast to starboard, as the steamer assumed a "middle-of-the-road" course down the lake. The island archipelago, with subdued Lake Michigan waves lapping against its shorelines, was a familiar "water guide" which skippers used to establish nautical positions. Had Captain Bryan been able to foresee the incredible metamorphosis the November weather would undergo on the return trip home, he would have sworn it was an alien sea.

Once the longest ship on the Great Lakes, the *S/S Carl D. Bradley* was the pride of the fleet. Here the vessel is shown near the Soo Locks. (Calcite Screenings)

But now the sea was cooperative and calm. The skipper was also ever-mindful of an unwritten law of the Lakes: "Constant vigilance is the price of staying afloat." That caution would pay off once more; the steamer reached its Indiana destination without incident. The limestone-laden freighter deposited its heavy load on the Indiana shore. The vessel's sudden loss of weight, twelve thousand tons, also removed a burden from the minds of crewmen. This was their last trip of the season! They were only thirty hours away from rest, relaxation, loved ones – a vacation from the sea.

~~~~ ☐ ~~~~

CHAPTER 4

"and a time to pluck up that which is planted . . . "
(Ecclesiastes, 3:2)

The November skies turned gloomy as the *Bradley* silently lay docked at its Indiana berth. The restless wind was beginning to increase as tireless Lake Michigan waves developed a characteristic rolling pattern. A storm was brewing. A general "rule of thumb" on the Great Lakes is that it takes three days for a storm to blow in and another three days to blow itself out.

When the long, gray ship sailed away from its dock on November 17, the wind-driven waves had been building steadily, yet the breakers weren't uncharacteristic of what the proud vessel had weathered many times before. By nightfall the southwesterly wind increased its velocity, persistently whipping the greenish, toiling waves, which now broke cold warnings over a proud bow. Darkness smothered the ship as it continued a homeward journey.

The next morning revealed the storm was getting worse. Gale warnings had been posted as smaller craft, scurrying like skittering water bugs, sought safe havens. It became readily apparent to Captain Bryan and the crew that a major blow was forthcoming.

A following sea was developing. The seasoned crew respectfully regarded the building seas; they realized it might cause a minor delay in their arrival home. The men remained confident in their ship and skipper. One is reminded of Irish poet Thomas Moore's observation, "If there is one thing which impresses me more than another regarding that puny object, man, it is a ship under full sail, bearing with her trusting and hoping hearts."

The lake giant was riding the ever-cresting, wind-whipped

waves quite well, mainly because Captain Bryan had counteracted her lack of cargo by carrying some nine thousand tons of water ballast. A loaded ship can take more sea; an empty vessel rides high and takes a worse beating. During the morning of November 18, Bryan kept the steamer to the western side of Lake Michigan to take advantage of the protection afforded by the Wisconsin shore line. He maintained this course, varying from five to twelve miles offshore, until 2:00 p.m., when the ship's gyro heading was altered to 046 degrees true.

(*Author's Note: The* Bradley's *position was about ten miles from the Wisconsin shore and just off Cana Island when the ship's course was altered.*) It was time to direct the *Bradley* homeward! The vessel was beginning its trek across northern Lake Michigan and into violent history.

As the 638-foot giant started its swing into a long arc toward the top of a turbulent lake, it was to follow the regular ship channel located in the mid-center of Lake Michigan. The persistent, relentless wind inched higher, angrily lashing mounting waves against the long, gray hull. Still, the steamer, sailing at fourteen to fifteen knots, evenly rode the increasingly tempestuous turbulence. The churning, following sea seemed only to urge the great vessel homeward.

The afternoon inched its way toward an inevitable rendezvous with darkness. Captain Bryan, aware the turn from Lake Michigan toward Lake Huron would subject the ship to heavy weather broadside, requested that the cooks prepare an early dinner. This would allow time for the mess crew to clean up and secure quarters prior to the homeward turn.

The ship continued its roller-coaster-like ride with no hint of laboring. She was riding the swelling sea so well that the forward crew, avoiding the tunnel which normally was used as a precautionary measure in rough weather, walked the deck to the dining room, located in the aft section. The mess room was particularly active, full of bantering crewmen who seemed especially attentive, as this was their last shipboard supper of the season. The hamburgers, french fries, cold tomatoes, peaches and sponge cake somehow seemed tastier as the ship continued its homeward rush. Dinner was served without attaching the sideboards to the tables, a normal precaution if rough weather warranted it. After finishing supper, some crewmen retired to warm cabins while others relieved sailors who were on duty.

The *Bradley's* bow plunges through a twenty-five-foot breaker the fateful night of November 18, 1958.
(*Mayday! Mayday!* -- Kenneth E. Friedrich)

Bryan prepared the great ship for its "final kick" home. Pleased with the ship's weathering of the gale, Captain Bryan radioed Central Radio and Telegraph in Rogers City. The *Bradley* master said "all was well" aboard the ship. He estimated the steamer would dock at Calcite at two o'clock in the morning. Bryan set aside the radio mike and prepared to navigate the ship through the howling tempest building around them. It wouldn't be long now. They were only one hundred miles from home! But the witch of November was at hand.

The steamer was nearing the Beaver Island archipelago as it churned through protesting water some forty-seven miles northwest of Charlevoix, Michigan. The navigational charts revealed a water depth of more than three hundred feet. In another hour, the ship would be in the leeward side of the islands and in quieter seas.

But that hour would be lost to the ages, and the *Carl D. Bradley* would never again touch the calmer, familiar waters of Lake Huron. As the ship plowed a drifting sea, the howling storm was becoming excruciatingly louder and rougher. Dark, angry clouds scudded recklessly, aimlessly, across a dirty, cluttered sky. Spraying, frothing waves showered the vessel. The steel cables wailed a discordant, metallic refrain as a rushing, scolding wind whirled around the *Bradley's* undulating hull.

(Author's Note: The jet stream was much farther south than normal for November in 1958. As a result of this anomaly, a strong low pressure system formed through the high plains. The Lake Michigan storm intensified rapidly between November 17 and 18, causing very strong winds over Lake Michigan.)

"I made my way forward in the tunnel, and I
could see the old ship working,
moving right before my eyes."
– Frank Mays, *Bradley* Deck Watchman

At 5:26 p.m., First Mate Elmer Fleming, on watch with the skipper and wheelsman in the pilot house, answered a call from Central Radio and Telegraph in Rogers City. Radio operator Frank E. Sager related a routine message which Fleming acknowledged. The first mate said nothing of any difficulty on the storm-tossed ship. Unknown to Fleming and the rest of the crew, the *Bradley* was already in the initial stages of its death throes, although the ship gave little evidence it was succumbing to the relentless attack of the swirling November gale.

(*Author's Note: From 1936 to 1939 Frank E. Sager, a native of Warren, Ohio, sailed as a radio operator aboard the* Bradley.)

Deck watchman Frank Mays went to the unloading tunnel to attend to some routine chores. After a load of limestone was deposited, the ship's deck and cargo holds had to be washed down. Mays started a pump that carried off water accumulation and bits of stone in the bottom of the vessel. Finished with the familiar "sumping out" procedure, Frank started walking through the tunnel, between the two conveyors, toward the forward end of the ship.

Suddenly – briefly – a strange noise alerted his senses. He stopped and listened. Nothing. *Hmm, must be that imagination again.* Mays would recall the sound later. In fact, Frank would remember it for the rest of his life.

The clock ticked toward 5:30 p.m. as Captain Roland Bryan, First Mate Elmer Fleming, and Wheelsman Raymond Kowalski stood guard in the pilot house. The gale that engulfed their ship was not a place for the meek or fainthearted. Outside was a building, devastating, wintry storm that most would reserve for an adventure story. The raging storm, inexorably, was getting worse. Sixty-five mile-per-hour winds inched ever-higher. Crashing, spraying, frothing white caps smashed relentlessly against the steel hull of the wallowing vessel.

The rushing waves and battering wind seemed like some mighty, allied cosmic sword, stealthily probing for the *Bradley's* Achilles' heel, while mutually threatening to deliver a fatal blow. And a waiting, weathered, conspiratorial eye, swirling angrily from above, decided it was time.

~~~~~ ☐ ~~~~~

CHAPTER 5

"a time to break down . . .
(Ecclesiastes, 3:3)

The *Bradley* **smashed through a raging hell.** In a storm-tossed pilot house, three men were attempting to guide their water-soaked vessel through crashing waves. The roar was deafening, but it failed to disguise another sound. A sickening, unnatural noise alerted the men. **THUD!** What the – ! They quickly spun around and looked down the long deck. A strange but alarming sight confronted them. Christ! . . . **BANG!** The stern was uncharacteristically low. It was sagging horribly!

"I heard a heavy 'thud' from somewhere in the ship, and an alarm bell began to clang. I spun around and looked back aft down the deck. I saw the stern of the boat was sagging and knew we were in trouble." – Elmer Fleming

"I heard a BANG – loudest noise I ever heard."
– Frank Mays

Seamen have a "sixth sense" as to the nature of maritime disaster. And the men in the pilot house knew their ship was in serious trouble. Deck watchman Mays was in the forward conveyor room with deckhand Gary Price when they heard the same, doomsday-like warning. They rushed topside! Captain Bryan quickly ordered Fleming to transmit a Mayday message. His ship was in serious trouble, and the skipper hoped rescue operations could be started as soon as possible. Rushing winds and turbulent waves continued to assault the stricken ship.

At 5:31 p.m., maritime radio operators were startled when they heard what sounded like a "Mayday" distress call. "Mayday" is a term familiar to any marine-oriented person. It is derived from the French word "M'aidez," which means "help me." First Mate Elmer Fleming's shrill voice rang out over marine Channel 51.

"Mayday! Mayday! Mayday! *Carl D. Bradley* breaking in two and going down twelve miles southwest of Gull Island . . . any ships in vicinity, please come!" Fleming's initial plea almost went unheard. It was partially drowned out by station static and inconsequential dispatches of marine radio operators. But Marine Radio Station WAD at Port Washington, Wisconsin, had heard Fleming's desperate call (as did station NMD at Chesterfield, Ohio).

"This is an emergency! This is an emergency!
Clear the channel!"
– WAD station operator Roy Brunette

Fleming's rising voice again crackled through the airwaves. "Mayday! Mayday! This is the *Carl D. Bradley*! Our position is approximately twelve miles southwest of Gull Island! We are in serious trouble!" Startled midwestern radio operators listened in shocked and subdued silence as they heard Captain Bryan's terse orders, against the backdrop of Fleming's plea, as the skipper exhorted crew members to initiate life saving measures.

"Run! Grab your life jackets!" Bryan screamed. "Get your life jackets!" Fleming continued to yell into the radio mike. The ship "thudded" once more. Elmer Fleming was aghast as the stern heaved heavily. "Mayday! This is the *Carl D. Bradley*, about twelve miles southwest of Gull Island! The ship is breaking up in heavy seas! We're breaking up! We're going to sink! We're going down!"

The verbs were prophetically accurate. The scene evolved into madness, an impending doom. A general alarm rang loudly on the ship! Quickly, the skipper used the Chadburn to signal the stopping of now-useless engines. Aware that something was terribly wrong as the carrier lurched in the crashing crescendo, crewmen began racing for their lives! Captain Bryan, in one of his last acts as captain, blew seven blasts of the ship's whistle, followed by one long one. Seamen instantly recognized the "abandon ship" signal, which shrieked hauntingly in the slashing storm. No routine drill this time! The men were in full flight.

The beginning of the end of the *Bradley*.
(*Mayday! Mayday!* – Kenneth E. Friedrich)

"I looked aft along the port side and saw the stern of the *Bradley* swinging up and down, just as your hand swings your wrist at the end of your arm . . ." – Frank Mays

As the impersonal, swirling November gale continued its deadly assault, the *Bradley* assumed an almost-human character. It lurched and moaned, futilely resisting the unyielding might of nature's unharnessed anger. The demanding wind snapped the vessel's power cables like a dry twig being crushed underfoot. The cables, unfamiliarly unattached, flailed uncontrollably in the high winds, whipping the storm as if in stubborn protest to its impending devastation.

With the *Bradley's* forward lights out and radio dead, the ship thudded and creaked once more. The proud ship was suffering a violent death as raging, storm-tossed waters eagerly waited to invade the emptiness of its vulnerable holds.

First Mate Fleming stared at the terror. The cables whipped uselessly across the deck. Elmer tossed aside the dead radiophone. Couldn't do much more there! Quickly, he glanced around. *Jesus! Not a life preserver in sight!*

A taut-faced fellow crewman hurried up to Fleming and handed him a ring buoy. But that wouldn't help much against the frothing, monstrous waves. Elmer Fleming raced below deck to his stateroom, donned an orange-colored life jacket, and raced back to the main deck. All hell had broken loose as the *Bradley* reluctantly yielded to a devastating onslaught.

THUD! Fleming looked down a once-proud deck. The ship seemed so confused. It shuddered violently once more, creating reverberating shock waves. He surmised she would let go somewhere between its tenth and eleventh hatches. *Maybe I could get to the –* Suddenly, he was pitched headlong into the lake.

The deafening stormy madness rose to a feverish new pitch, the moment of catastrophe appeared to be briefly suspended in time, and the angry devastation reached its pinnacle of cruel triumph. It seemed as if the stern had been reaching out for the bow. But it wasn't there anymore.

~~~~ ☐ ~~~~

CHAPTER 6

"and a time to die . . . "
(Ecclesiastes, 3:2)

Elmer Fleming was thrown into a raging sea as the bow
lurched violently, plunging rapidly into a stormy wake. Moments
earlier he had seen Captain Bryan and several crewmen pulling
themselves along the railing of the heavily listing bow. Now they
were nowhere to be seen.

(*Author's Note: In the U.S. Coast Guard's final report, the*
Bradley's *alarm sounded, and the crew responded quickly; most
sought to abandon the ship. With the exception of the second mate,
who tried to go aft toward the boat deck, those forward donned life
jackets and went to the fifteen-man emergency life raft aft of the pilot
house. Men aft were observed on the boat deck, lowering the
starboard lifeboat. The two lifeboats were twenty-five-person boats
on the boat deck aft, equipped with quadrant-type mechanical davits,
Manila falls, and common hooks.*)

**"The last picture I had was that the two parts of the
vessel had separated, and I had a passing glimpse
directly into the stern end.
It was moving to port while the bow section, which I was
aboard, was moving to starboard and sagging aft."**
–Elmer Fleming

Spraying, cold water swirled around Fleming, as driving,
wintry winds forced air temperatures down into the chilling thirties.
Wind gusts approaching seventy miles-per-hour lashed the hellish

lake, creating twenty-foot, monstrous, foaming waves, and the proverbial "seventh wave" cresting at thirty feet. Fleming glanced wildly about! He noticed a fellow crewman who floated precariously nearby. It looked like Frank Mays.

Swirling waters engulfed the men! They looked uncertainly around. Spraying waves blurred their vision and splashed icy water on shocked senses. It felt like a million springs were rushing through their bodies. They felt so alone. Nowhere to go. Rushing, rolling waves, eager to control their destiny.

When Fleming surfaced after his icy plunge, he was about two feet from the forward life raft, which had floated free after the *Bradley* began its plunge into the dark, disturbed water. Clad in a life preserver and fleeced, foul-weather gear, Elmer Fleming awkwardly climbed aboard. Crewman Frank Mays, wearing a life preserver, khaki trousers, and fleeced foul weather gear, resurfaced after his brief underwater descent. Mays discovered he was about four feet from that same forward raft, so he painfully climbed on.

Other crewmen also saw the bobbing raft in the stormy distance, but they were much farther away. Still, the men desperately swam toward the raft. Resisting waves hindered their progress. It almost seemed as though the waves were reasoning, sadistically thinking of cruel ways to increase the distance between the men and their one hope for survival. Howling, scolding winds aided the waves in the attempt. But the witch showed some mercy for Fleming and Mays. They, at least, were out of the frigid waters of Lake Michigan.

In strange irony, however, Fleming and Mays, who so often had walked massive, non-skid decks to earn a living, now were clinging to a slippery, confining 8-by-10-foot "home" as they fought for survival. Both stared in transfixed horror and disbelief as they saw the ship's stern rise, propeller out of the tall water, and plunge with brutal finality to a forbidding resting place 360 feet below the raging lake. An explosion followed as the icy, Lake Michigan waters found the hot boilers.

"It went down by its open end and didn't roll. There was an explosion from the stern as I was getting on the raft. The forward end was already down, and the blast came just as the aft end was disappearing.

"It was a white flame with a terrific jet force. I can't tell  about the smoke; I didn't see any, and it would have been carried away very quickly in that wind. I have a picture in my mind of a jet plane crash, just that quick. It lit up the area when it went off." – Elmer Fleming

Above: A 'gray lady' goes down, November 18, 1958.
(*Mayday! Mayday!* – Kenneth E. Friedrich)

Two huddled, shivering, frightened men witnessed a macabre scene. The sea was boiling in the *Bradley's* plunging wake, cries for help from drifting crewmen pierced the howling wind, tall waves wildly pitched ring buoys, their tiny lights casting a ghost-like, spectral glow in the approaching darkness. The men scanned the violent turmoil. They saw distant crewmen who had escaped the ship before it had slipped into the sea. Fleming and Mays started yelling, trying to overcome screaming winds and crashing waves.

"Over here!" they yelled. "We're over here!" Rushing winds and rolling waves mocked them as they continued loud pleas to attract the attention of their sailor buddies. Cries for help were getting fainter. One of the pleas belonged to deck watchman Gary Strzelecki, who managed to swim through the turmoil toward the raft. Fleming and Mays clumsily pulled him aboard.

The three men tried to attract the others' attention, but the surrounding, hellish treachery engulfing them was serving cruel notice – *it* was now in command. Helpless crewmen, separated from the raft by mountainous waves and approaching darkness, would have to take their chances with the god-forsaken witch.

"The sea was so great that men were hidden."
– Elmer Fleming

As weakening pleas for help grew mercilessly fainter, one more crewman was awkwardly pulled aboard the raft. Dennis Meredith, a *Bradley* deckhand, had been enjoying the warmth of his bunk when he heard the general alarm. Now, shoeless and wearing light trousers and a heavy, white sweatshirt, he was cold and terrified as the life raft floated precariously on the swollen sea.

The four men tightly gripped the drenched, tossing raft as deathly waters threatened to sweep them into an unending maritime nightmare. Fleming somehow managed to open a hatch, which contained several flares, among other life saving gear. The oars were swept into the raging sea, where they floated like lifeless corks on cresting, crashing waves. They wouldn't be of much use anyway. The storm was doing the steering. Fleming fired several flares shortly after the sinking, saving one of them for close-approaching rescuers . . . if there were any.

Meanwhile, Fleming's final Mayday dispatch was touching off a desperate, extensive search-and-rescue effort by the U.S. Coast Guard. At a five-story tower overlooking the gale-swept lake at Charlevoix, Michigan, Fireman 1/c Charles Pettit was on radio watch. Pettit, along with Boatswain's Mate 1/c Edward Basset, was monitoring radio dispatches when the distress call was received. The men urgently tried to tell Fleming help was on the way. But they didn't know if their message was received. The last words they had heard from the stricken ship were that, "We're going down!"

Basset quickly jumped down a ladder, nearly breaking his leg in the process. He quickly alerted Chief Officer Joseph Etienne. The senior officer, immediately and automatically, commenced the often-used, time-honored life saving search-and-rescue machinery of the nation's oldest military service. Etienne realized the gargantuan task that confronted the Coast Guard as he observed horrid weather conditions.

Huge waves battered Charlevoix's shoreline; high-velocity winds had shredded one of the red flags flying above the Coast Guard station; occasional blasts of snow squalls reminded him it was indeed November as the rushing wind hurled cold snow against shuddering windows, which rattled loudly as if pelted by buckshot. And the visibility – or lack of it – was appalling.

On a clear day it was possible to see the hump of Beaver Island from Charlevoix. But not this day. The dirty sky and tall water conspired to raise havoc with the lake as they obliterated the jagged "Christmas tree" effect of waves on a now-lost horizon. Etienne wistfully surmised rescue chances would be slim that day, yet he pressed on with determined purposefulness.

~~~ ❑ ~~~

CHAPTER 7

"a time to weep . . ."
(Ecclesiastes, 3:4)

Lake Michigan. A vivid illustration of terror. Slightly disturbed only twenty-four hours earlier. Now at war with itself. Screaming winds. Invading, choking darkness. Crashing, turbulent waves battling for supremacy, creating ear-shattering anger, warning any intruders that death was only a violent motion away.

Another ship dared to sail through the hell-engulfed waves. The *Christian Sartori*, a 250-foot German vessel, had been en route to Chicago; Captain Paul Mueller, one-time German U-boat officer, had been observing the *Bradley's* troubled progress. The *Christian Sartori,* about thirteen degrees off the *Bradley's* port bow, was only four miles from the distressed carrier. A stunned Captain Mueller had watched the ship vanish from the sea. The wind and waves continued a hellish assault on the *Christian Sartori*, battering the vessel with great force.

(Author's Note: The only side light seen at any time by the captain and crewmen of the Christian Sartori *was the* Carl D. Bradley's *red light (port-side); at no time was the ship's green side light (starboard-side) visible to the* Christian Sartori.*)

Immediately, Mueller diverted course and sailed toward the devastation. Normally, the vessel would have traversed the distance in fifteen minutes. But witches are far from normal. Slashing seas and gale-force winds hindered Mueller's progress for ninety minutes.

Earlier the *Christian Sartori's* crew had observed several, distant flares fired in the wreckage vicinity. That meant survivors had managed to escape the sinking ship. But it seemed the *Christian Sartori* was on a treadmill, unable to make much progress. The severe, objecting elements were serving notice that its anger precluded any possibility of an immediate rescue. A wide-eyed Captain Mueller continued his assault against the damnable witch.

Finally arriving at a windswept, wave-dominated scene, German crewmen saw grim evidence of the wreckage – a tank and a raincoat – float lifelessly by. The *Sartori's* probing searchlight cut through gloomy darkness like an eerie specter, a maritime ghost. Concerned sailors strained their worried eyes to locate signs of life, but a Stygian, black veil cloaked the scene. Sadly, reluctantly, Captain Mueller radioed a terse message to the Coast Guard.

"I believe all hands are lost . . . no lifeboats are visible." The *Christian Sartori* continued its crisscross pattern over tall, angry waters. The heavily rolling ship's headway was very slow. Its searchlight located only mocking waves and lifeless wisps of wind-blown, November snow. Mueller, with a heavy German accent, told the Coast Guard, "In six years of sailing the Great Lakes, I have never seen such rough waters."

The death of the
Carl D. Bradley
(Sarah Altman)

The Coast Guard asked Mueller whether he could determine what had caused the great steamer to go down. The German master reported that when he first had observed the *Bradley*, it was "wallowing heavily," when Mueller saw what appeared to be an explosion. "It seemed to be forward of the engine space and to the rear of the cargo section . . . it was a heavy fire . . . a very bright light. . .and then it was all dark, and the ship was hidden by clouds of black smoke."

(*Author's Note: The eruption of steam and combustion as the* Bradley *sank gave the mistaken impression to witnesses on the* Christian Sartori *that the* Bradley *had exploded.*)

As the *Christian Sartori* continued a cold, lonely search, the Charlevoix Coast Guard's dispatching of ships to the rescue area was understandably difficult. Seamen Dan Routtinen, Seth Southard, and Huie Brizendian piloted a thirty-six-foot lifeboat onto the stormy lake. It was like floating a toothpick in a tossing swimming pool. The brave men were forced back after making only four miles "headway" in the hellish gale. The raging storm had already proven itself a ship killer; yet the seamen were willing to risk the same elements which earlier had torn a lake giant in two.

Lt. Commander Harold Muth also showed great courage. The Coast Guard veteran, who had issued an emergency recall to those he had granted shore leave, headed out onto Lake Michigan with less than two-thirds of his forty-man crew. He was carefully guiding the 180-foot cutter *Sundew* through the brewing witch.

Another cutter, the *Hollyhock*, was en route from Sturgeon Bay, Wisconsin, to assist in rescue operations. These Coast Guard cutters were designated as buoy tenders, which have low-sided, forward decks, to enable the deployment and retrieval of navigational buoys. The low freeboard made the cutters valuable in case crewmen spotted survivors floating in the water.

(*Author's note: When the* Bradley's *distress call was received, the* Sundew *was moored at the Coast Guard Buoy Depot, in a small channel between Round Lake and Lake Charlevoix. Normally, the cutter would sail through the open railroad bridge in Lake Charlevoix, turn around, then go back through the bridge into Round Lake. The* Sundew *would blow its signal to open the bridge before heading toward Lake Michigan.*

But Lt. Commander Muth had trouble getting back through the railroad bridge's opening because of strong winds. High gusts kept blowing the vessel off course; in order to reach the opening at just the right moment – and at the correct speed – the Sundew *had to proceed at an angle to accomplish the maneuver. Considering the nature of the November 18, 1958, storm, many believed the* Sundew *would not return.)*

The seas were dark; its hull broke deep, as water claimed her soul.

Captaining his understaffed vessel toward beckoning, open water, Lt. Commander Muth learned, not surprisingly, that several small rescue craft from the Beaver Island and Charlevoix life boat stations were forced back due to life-threatening weather. Muth continued his courageous journey through the horrendous holocaust. Finally, at approximately 10:40 p.m., the *Sundew* arrived at the disaster scene and began assisting the *Christian Sartori* in search patterns. The *Hollyhock* joined them later. The three search vessels continued to scan the area where a ship that eclipsed their entire lengths was lying as a broken hulk below. The rescue ships, rolling some fifty degrees in the tall water, were not alone.

The Traverse City Air Station recorded winds of fifty-eight and sixty miles-per-hour, with wind gusts approaching sixty-eight miles-per-hour on open waters. Nevertheless, a two-engine Grumman Albatross sea plane took off over double, triangular red flags at Traverse City. The crew hoped to aid rescue attempts by dropping parachute flares to provide a degree of visibility.

The huge waves, offended by the intrusion of bright lights on its stormy domain, quickly doused the magnesium flares, leaving little time for them to remain lit. The pilot conducted four flights, dropping some 88 high-intensity flares before being forced back to home base because of dangerous gusts and exhaustion of flares. Wind gusts approaching one hundred miles-per-hour buffeted the small plane at its higher altitudes, frequently causing the aircraft to drop two hundred feet at a time.

The rescue ships continued lonely search vigils. Crewmen were getting weary yet pressed on. No one could sleep in the deafening storm. Crashing waves pushed ships around at will, proudly demonstrating its violent force. Back at Charlevoix, Michigan, Chief Etienne was receiving dreaded negative reports. *No. No trace of the crew. Only a few bits of wreckage.*

Contemplating search efforts, Etienne muttered, "Lots of boys out there tonight being hammered into men." He joined other Coast Guardsmen for a forthcoming, long wait. Among the uniforms, storm jackets and blue jeans, a young man somehow seemed out of place.

"What's your interest in this?" he was asked. "My brother Marty's out there," John Enos replied. "He's a stoker on the *Bradley*. I was supposed to pick him up in Rogers City at 2:00 a.m., but when I got the news, I drove over here to Charlevoix. This is the place to meet him now. He'll be coming in here." Assembled reporters quickly crowded around the young man, who smilingly mentioned that Marty (Clyde) Enos was going to get married in Cheboygan after the shipping season. The Coast Guardsmen silently turned away.

~~~~~ □ ~~~~~
CHAPTER 8

" a time to mourn . . ."
(Ecclesiastes, 3:4)

The ominous news came around suppertime. The initial realization of disaster struck Rogers City like a giant, cosmic lightning bolt. The *Bradley*? Down in Lake Michigan? No! That's impossible! What in God's name had happened? There were conflicting rumors. *Yes, the ship had sunk, and all were lost. No, the* Bradley *was down in Lake Michigan, but the crew had made it to an island.* No one was really sure about anything.

Few slept as house lights burned brightly, eternal flames throughout an endless night, offering mute testimony to the beginning vigil that would seem an eternity. Most remained sequestered in the isolated loneliness of their homes, while others sought the aid and comfort of friends. Many were beginning an intense emotional battle.

Another kind of struggle was being waged on the angry waters of Lake Michigan. Not content to have claimed a monster freighter, the merciless, raging elements continued its assault on the *Bradley's* small forward life raft. Four weary sailors were beginning, what was to be, an all-night battle for survival. Chilled to the bone by raw winds and icy waters, the men stubbornly and steadfastly held on for dear life.

When the *Christian Sartori* appeared on the disaster scene, four hopeful souls happily, yet cautiously, observed its approach. It appeared as though the German vessel, whose lights danced crazily on the tall water, was heading straight for them! Suddenly, unexpectedly, a great, crashing wave swamped the raft, sweeping the men into the death-beckoning lake! Icy water again swirled around their resisting, weakening bodies. In the inky blackness and drowning din, Elmer Fleming made it back to the raft first. Gary Strzelecki, Frank Mays and Dennis Meredith somehow managed to follow him.

"The *Sartori* appeared to be coming straight toward us when a wave swamped the raft." -- Elmer Fleming

They quickly looked to see whether the ship was still visible. To their relief, the *Christian Sartori* still was heading toward them! The sailors tried to rivet their blurred vision on the German ship, but the wild, pitching raft, and the shock waves which raced through them after their icy plunge, made it almost possible to concentrate on two things at once. The *Christian Sartori* continued the approach, its searchlight cutting a ghostly image into the seemingly dark nothingness. Once the light swept by the raft, briefly revealing the men. But the limited visibility its beam afforded didn't show anything that attracted attention.

My God! We're close enough to almost reach out and touch the ship! "Hey! Over here!" they screamed. German crewmen heard only howling winds and crashing waves. Dismay pervaded the men's thoughts.

Jesus! They aren't stopping! They can't hear us! Fleming then remembered the last flare he had saved for such a moment. It was an opportune time to light it, and crewmen on the *Christian Sartori's* deck surely would see its bright glow. Believing a rescue would be at hand once the device was lit, Fleming was horrified to learn the signal flare was being sadistically uncooperative. He couldn't get the damned thing open! Fleming desperately tore at it with his teeth. *Come on! Not now!*

His shaking, freezing fingers finally managed to prepare the flare for firing. But to Elmer's dismay the flare cruelly refused to ignite, having been dampened by laughing waves. Sagging, defeated shoulders "watched" as the *Christian Sartori* was swallowed by darkness. Their hopes dashed by continued bad luck, the men huddled for warmth on their cramped home. Rescue, so close yet so distant, was gone for the moment. Although invigorated by rescue hopes, the seamen were reminded of the harsh coldness, which returned to assault their weakening bodies, a parasite hungrily feeding on its host. It would be so easy to let go. To fade into abysmal oblivion. Yet they tenaciously and instinctively held on! Fleming berated himself for not wearing long underwear.

The long night crept by. Frank Mays hung doggedly on as the sea crashed angrily around him. It was so damned cold! Probing, penetrating coldness. Suddenly Frank felt a strange sensation on the top of his head. He dared to free a clutching, freezing hand.

Oh my God! Ice! The damned water was freezing! An immediate check of his jacket revealed crusts of coldness. Freezing ice meant numb hands. And with no feeling in their hands, they surely would lose the ability to clutch the sides of the tossing raft. Hell, they could even stay on the raft all night, only to be dead of exposure by morning. If there was a hell on earth, then this had to be it. But help was on the way! It just had to be . . .

Four weary, weakened voices began mutual encouragement, realizing they, at least, had a chance for survival when so many of their fellow crewmen were seemingly beyond help. "Don't go to sleep, men!" Fleming exhorted them. "Don't go to sleep, or you're a goner!" Dennis Meredith was in the worst physical shape. Scantily dressed, extremely cold, numb and tired, he was showing immutable signs of giving in to the elements. Immediately, the other three clumsily massaged his shivering body to stimulate circulation.

"Move your legs! Come on, you can do it!" . . . **"I don't know whether he heard me. He wasn't unconscious, but I don't think I was getting to him."** -- Elmer Fleming

──────

One of them offered, "Let's count to make sure we don't go to sleep! One! Two! Three!" Three quivering voices joined in the cadence. Meredith remained silent. Sometime during the angry night, another large wave crested under the raft, sending the exhausted, tired men into the lake again. Flipped off of their one life hope once more, the sailors frantically swam for the raft.

"It (the wave) was so high we went straight up into the air." – Elmer Fleming

"At times we were better off in the water; the lake was warmer than the air temperature."
– Frank Mays

A scornful sea smashed into them, furiously resisting their efforts. Mays reached the overturned raft first. A shivering Gary Strzelecki soon joined him. Fleming, who was trapped briefly under the raft, managed to claw his way aboard.

Just one more, God, just one more!

Suddenly Dennis Meredith also reappeared, but – being the worst dressed for the hellish weather – was too weak to climb aboard the raft. Mays and Strzelecki helped Meredith hold onto the raft. The wind howled its curses. The sea crashed angrily around them. The storm gods had their way, lashing and slashing, the epitome of hellish dreams. It seemed as though that November gale was consuming itself – again and again, a storm of storms.

Meredith continued to weaken. His vision dimmed; his arms relaxed. The freezing wind and water were too much. The sea claimed his soul. Dennis Meredith was twenty-five years old.

There emerged a tomblike silence. And, for a time, Fleming, Mays, and Strzelecki became impervious to the curse around them. But no hope there. No clinical cure for the human suffering that moment.

Once she rode the Lakes so grandly, broad banner waving proudly, as the *Bradley* sailed through the Soo Locks on its maiden voyage in 1927. Now she sits quietly on Lake Michigan's floor, resting serenely while her sister ships ply restless seas. (*Calcite Screenings*)

Memories of an Echo

Youth and age sail on a sea,
riding on hopes and prayers.
Storm and wind batter a soul, tear a ship,
then slip away.
Secrets abound, answers hidden,
bubbling depth, sand and silt,
An echo calls, memories stir;
we take it to heart, take it too hard.
Imagine in peace.
– *James L. Hopp*

~~~~ ❑ ~~~~
CHAPTER 9

"and a time to gather stones together . . ."
(Ecclesiastes, 3:5)

The cruelness refused to disappear. Gary Strzelecki tried valiantly to renew their tortured spirits. Gary was an excellent swimmer. As another rushing, crashing wave came rolling toward the raft, he would shout, "Here comes another big one, fellows! Get set!"

But the cursed witch slowly, methodically, was sapping their weakening strength. More body massages and counting cadences, their hoarse voices heard only by the callous, crashing sea. Later Gary Strzelecki, perhaps overcome by delirium, mutely expressed a desire to swim. He left the raft and started swimming. The storm continued its madness. Fleming and Mays were now alone. Where does the Grace of God go when the wait turns minutes to hours?

Only two left. Elmer Fleming and Frank Mays huddled together on their reckless home. Thoughts of Dennis Meredith and Gary Strzelecki haunted them. *Would I be next?* A large, crashing breaker rudely interrupted their fears. Yet they hung on with determination. The men dared to speculate about rescue attempts; they knew ships were in the vicinity. But hellish elements made nighttime attempts very difficult and hazardous. If they could only make it to daylight! Was that too much to ask? A cold, spraying mist was the witches' reply, as it hung around, a hovering, damned albatross, cruelly reminding all its job was not finished. The night wore on; the raft drifted aimlessly in stormy sadness.

The extensive, hampered Coast Guard searches continued. Rough seas, high winds, snow squalls and haunting darkness remained deadly deterrents. The *S/S Robert C. Stanley* arrived to offer assistance. Its appearance was greeted by the swirling November gale. James Cropper, in command of the *Hollyhock*, gave the final words as to the nature of that stealing autumn witch.

"It was the roughest sea I ever saw, and I've seen quite a few. At times, the pitching and the rolling and the valleys were so deep, it looked like the water was going uphill in front of us. The ocean men kid us lake men about our 'little ponds', but I better never hear that again. Last night was a visit to hell."

The darkness crawled on, a wounded snake. More crashing waves. Scolding winds. Maritime terror unfolding like some classic, storybook sea adventure. But a ray of hope. The witch was tiring, although not without reluctance. Incredibly, almost imperceptibly, there was a thin line of light beginning to peek out on the dirty horizon. *Jesus, Mary and Joseph.* Dawn was mercifully approaching. Tiring Coast Guard teams welcomed the arrival of the dim light. Now they could see! Weary, squinting eyes scanned the sea. Floating debris. Still more, floating without purpose or direction. A huge, trailing oil slick spread out over subdued waves.

The seas were dying, although the faded witch took a few parting shots as it lashed some smashing breakers in defiant triumph against weathered hulls. Once-violent winds were now almost infant-like as thirty-mile-per-hour gusts played tag with the waves. Search planes were dispatched from Selfridge and Kinross air force bases. A Navy PV2 sea plane was en route from the Glenville Naval Air Station. Their movements made easier by the dying storm, search teams again began the arduous task of scanning the sea for signs of wreckage, and, hopefully, survivors.

In Rogers City the long night faded into day. There were more definitive reports coming in from the Coast Guard: *The* Bradley *had sunk in Lake Michigan during a violent storm. Ships, planes and helicopters were on the scene. There were no signs yet of the thirty-five-man crew.* The small town was becoming the center of nationwide scrutiny. Radios blared incessant reports of search and rescue operations, reminding listeners most crewmen were from Rogers City.

Newsmen throughout Michigan converged on the stricken community late Tuesday night when news of the sinking spread like an untrue rumor. The *Detroit Times, Detroit Free Press, Detroit News, The Alpena News, Bay City Times, Lansing State Journal, Life* and *Time* magazines – all sent reporters to secure details and interview families. Newspaper headlines painted a grim story.

Richard Allgire, a U.S. Steel Corporation director of public relations, established headquarters in Rogers City as he kept media and the community informed of the latest developments. The Advance Publishing Company's employees worked overtime, as their office remained open the long night of November 18th to relay stories to enquiring nationwide news agencies.

The task of disseminating information became almost too great. The great influx of news people resulted in additional public relations' officials being flown in from Duluth, Minnesota, and Cleveland, Ohio, to aid in handling news coverage.

(Author's Note: Life *magazine featured an eight-page spread about the* Bradley *sinking in its December 1, 1958, edition (STORM AND DEATH ON A GREAT LAKE). The spread showed a number of photographs, as well as a brief commentary about other lake disasters. The magazine's cover pictured singer Ricky Nelson with his guitar. A number of these magazines are still around. The author bought a copy on eBay for $18.50. To the people of Rogers City, the magazine is "priceless history."*

Time *magazine also covered the tragedy in its December 1, 1958, edition ("The Death of the Bradley"). The cover of* Time *for that issue featured Mao Tse-Tung, who would become one of China's most formidable leaders.)*

Above: The *Bradley* at Calcite. Before bow thrusters, Calcite vessels were guided by two tugs into a loading slip.

The Calcite tugs *Dolomite* [800-h.p. / steam-powered], and *Limestone* (left) [1,020-h.p. / diesel-electric-powered] were equipped with long and short-range radio. Both tugs were 94' long. The *Limestone* had a full-range radar used on trips to ports such as Cedarville.

(*Calcite Screenings*)

~~~~~ ▢ ~~~~~

CHAPTER 10

"a time to embrace . . ."
(Ecclesiastes, 3:5)

The long, cruel wait continued. Twenty-five wives and fifty-two living children anxiously waited for good news. Two women were expecting. Most were riveted to the radio. Many had maintained all-night vigils, their hearts leaping as they answered an inevitably ringing telephone. *No. Nothing yet. They're still looking.*

Patricia Gager had planned a thirty-candle birthday for her husband Cleland, a *Bradley* oiler. Gager's birthday had been on November 17, so Pat and her three children were anticipating a belated party. The candles remained unlit.

Gerald Greengtski was concerned over his brother Paul's safety. "I didn't expect that," he said in a subdued monotone. "Maybe there's a chance he's alive out there somewhere."

Mrs. Joseph Krawczak bravely hoped for her husband's safety. Cecelia's birthday had been on November 18. "I want to keep my spirits up for the children," she offered. "Already they want to know why their father hasn't come home for my party." She held a card Joe had mailed her a few days before. Cecelia would memorize it before the day was through. In the card he had written, "Here's a card that fits you just right, I guess. We were at Cedarville . . . man, did we have a roll coming over. " The birthday greeting read, "From the guy who seldom shows it but knows his wife is a whiz!" Joe Krawczak, a wheelsman, was the father of six children.

Two Rogers City men silently pondered the tragedy. Sylvester Sobeck and George Sobeck, Jr., would have been aboard the doomed freighter had not a strange, ironic twist occurred.

George, Jr., a porter, had left the *Bradley* two weeks earlier to be at the side of his dying father. His replacement was James Selke, a first-time traveler on the ship. Sylvester, an engineer, had departed the great vessel at Cedarville when news of his brother's death became known.

Friends and relatives of Douglas Bellmore waited for news. Flora Bellmore later revealed a letter her husband had sent a day before the sinking. "I'll see you Tuesday if nothing goes wrong," Doug had written. In the upper, left-hand corner of the envelope was a disturbing, and later prophetic, inscription – 'somewhere in Lake Michigan'. *(Author's Note: The Bellmore family had five sailor brothers: Douglas, 34, a* Bradley *porter; Robert, 27, wheelsman on the* Cedarville; *Leslie, 30, 2nd engineer,* W.F. White; *George, 43, stoker,* John G. Munson; *Stanley, 40, repairman,* Myron C. Taylor.*)*

Others clung to hope. One was my neighbor on First Street, Mrs. Marjorie Schuler, whose husband, Keith, had been sailing for eight years. She learned the news from a friend who had heard it on the radio. "I thought she was kidding," Mrs. Schuler related. "Then the news suddenly sank in. I'm still hoping because of my faith in God and in my husband."

Sharing her faith and long vigil were her children, Duwayne, 15, Randy, 11, and Jane, 6. Duwayne was a classmate and friend of my older brother, Neil. Randy was a childhood playmate who would conjure up pranks with me and my younger brother, Randy, at Lakeside Park. We weren't in a playful mood that day. Friendships and blood relationships ran deep in the community.

At bedtime Eleanore Tulgetske called her children, Karen, 6, Susan, 5, and Paul, 3, into her bedroom. Cradling Leslie, 14 months, in her arms, Eleanore led them in five "Hail Mary's" as their young voices followed hers as she prayed for her husband's (Earl Tulgetske) safety.

Ann Strzelecki slumped in a blue dress and bobby socks in a gray-shingled house. Her son, Benjamin, nine months, played busily on the floor. Gary Strzelecki's father, Benjamin, was very tired. He had been up all night as WHAK, the "Voice of the North," went off the air as Sault Ste. Marie's WSOO took over. "He wanted to get his family on its feet," Benjamin said. "As soon as the *Bradley* laid up, he was going to look for a home." A radio continued reporting sketchy, now-repetitious reports of the disaster. Gary's father was concerned, but his eyes reflected a steely glint. "Gary's a damn good swimmer," he said firmly. "I know he's going to make it."

Frances Vallee recalled her life in Detroit where her forty-nine-year-old husband Edward, a conveyorman, had worked as a milkman sixteen years ago. "We didn't like Detroit so we moved up here, and he's been sailing on the ships ever since. I wish we'd stayed in Detroit," she lamented.

Mrs. Raymond Buehler had extensive knowledge of the Lakes and their dangers. "My husband has worked on the Lakes for forty years," related Francis Buehler as she waited by the radio in Lakewood, Ohio, a Cleveland suburb. "I have been on all the ships with him many times. They can kick up a storm that will tear a ship to bits." Francis stated the last time she had seen Ray was in September, when the *Bradley* had docked at Cleveland. He had planned on returning home in December.

The Buehlers had one daughter, Bonny Ann, 19, a John Carroll University student. Mrs. Buehler recalled her husband's narrow, harrowing escape from a similar incident in 1919, when the freighter he was sailing on was blown nearly two hundred miles off course, during a violent Lake Huron gale.

"He told us water was waist-deep in the engine room, and none of the crew thought they'd get out alive." Then she reflected, "But he survived. This time things look even worse, but we are still hoping."

Another anxious relative, whose life had been tied to the Great Lakes, was Leo Fogelsonger of St. Ignace. His son, John, was a second mate on the sunken ship. Leo was a retired chief engineer on the Mackinac Straits ferries. "I thought I had seen the worst the Lakes could do; now I'm afraid they've taken my son," he said somberly.

Still others were in a state of understandable, severe shock.

Mrs. Mavis Kowalski, like her sister-in-law Ann Strzelecki, had a double concern over the tragedy. Her husband Raymond, a wheelsman, and brother, Gary Strzelecki, a deck watchman, were aboard the stricken ship. She informed her youngest son, Michael, about the sinking, but he was too young to comprehend the gravity of it all. Mavis and Ann continued a long, prayerful wait.

During the course of a lifetime, it seems people have unfailing memories as to where they were during the occurrence of a memorable event. When I went to the Rogers City Elementary School on the morning after the sinking, I recall sitting next to a classmate, Neil Jones, as we ate lunch in the gym. Our conversation wasn't ordinary.

Maybe, just maybe, the men had managed to escape the sinking steamer. Maybe they were all on an island, waiting to be rescued.

We didn't even know where Beaver Island was located, and we thought Carl D. Bradley was a crewman aboard his own ship. Maybe . . . The news had affected, and infected, the entire town. And there was little, so little, that could be done. Waiting was becoming difficult. Where does the Grace of God go when the wait turns minutes to hours?

~~~~ ❑ ~~~~

CHAPTER 11

"a time to keep . . ."
(Ecclesiastes, 3:6)

The **Bradley line had never lost a ship.** Until now. Grieved and distraught, Michigan Limestone President Christian F. Beukema, who had first heard the news while en route from Rogers City to Detroit, immediately returned to the stricken town to direct a disaster relief team. He assigned four officials to serve on a disaster relief committee (Norman Hoeft, George Jones, Blenn Cook, and Harold Jones). These men, along with Northern District president, Neil Patterson, were sent to crewmen's homes, where they offered assistance but cautioned against false hopes.

Roger Blough, chairman of the board of U.S. Steel Corporation, flew into Phelps Collins Air Field in Alpena, Michigan. Hurriedly, he drove to Rogers City to aid the disaster committee. Many planes arrived in Alpena.

Robert Welch, operator of Alpena Flying Service, reported that Phelps Collins' air traffic, occasioned by the Lake Michigan disaster, was "coming and going all the time." "Our parking ramp is filled up – we haven't got an open space on it," Welch said.

"We have over two million dollars worth of airplanes on the ramp right now." A four-engine Viscount, two Lockheed Learstars and a twin Beechcraft were readily identifiable on the plane-crowded ramp.

"Storm gods shrieked as the wind went mad and blew their dreams away . . . " *–James L. Hopp*

Michigan Limestone President Christian Beukema (left) and U.S. Steel Board Chairman Roger Blough await news about the fate of the *Carl D. Bradley*. (*Calcite Screenings*)

Newspapers across the country informed Americans of the disaster on Lake Michigan. The *Detroit News* printed sketchy details below a headline which read, "Grief Weights 4,000 Hearts in Rogers City"; the morning edition of Colorado's *Rocky Mountain News* stated, "Lake Michigan Ship is Lost and 35 are Believed Dead"; the main edition of the *Kansas City Star* reported it took search vessels "an hour to go three miles." Back on Lake Michigan the foreboding, still-swollen waters hampered search efforts. The storm had not been confined to the raging lake. Several Upper Peninsula communities were isolated when high winds toppled trees over power lines.

All telephone and teletype communications with the 'copper country' around Houghton and the Keweenaw Peninsula were knocked out by gale-force winds. The Detroit weather station reported wind velocities up to fifty-four miles-per-hour. Mountainous waves wrecked scores of boats while smashing summer cabins and resorts along Lake Superior's northern shore. And the third largest body of fresh water in America had swallowed a great limestone carrier, the worst shipping disaster in the history of the Great Lakes.

In the quieting seas, Elmer Fleming and Frank Mays floated aimlessly on their frozen home. Miraculously, they had made it through the raging night. Lake Michigan's waves, once instruments of violent destruction, now lapped almost apologetically against the raft's battered frame.

As the tiny speck floated uncertainly on the still-restless sea, a swollen, raw, cold Elmer Fleming, partially blinded by inky darkness and spraying waves, thought his weary, reddened eyes detected a trace of dawn. But he didn't believe it. Fleming was afraid to look up. Not another disappointment. He couldn't take it. With guarded realization that morning was indeed at hand, Fleming's eyes scanned the surrounding scenario.

A dark, angry-looking sky stared vacantly back at him. Subdued yet scornful waves blew against his weakened frame. As his forlorn eyes scanned a pitiless sky, the first mate thought he detected a distant movement. *Hey! It looks like a plane!*

Frank Mays, unnaturally puffy, peered up at the lonely sky. He told Fleming it was only a seagull. But then Mays painfully lifted his weary head again. Even a seagull would to be nice to look at. He was startled! The distant "seagull" had blinking lights!

Desperately, the sailors scrambled to rise! But the slippery surface and rolling waves made balance extremely difficult. Finally attaining a semblance of equilibrium, the swollen men realized they had nothing to signal with. Lethargic arms waved frantically. Hoarse voices pierced the iron coldness. Hope-filled eyes turned into a dismayed gaze. The men in the Coast Guard amphibian plane flying above the angry lake had failed to spot them. It droned away from the dispirited men below. Fleming and Mays sank in defeat. They settled down for more thinking. More drifting. More speculating about what *might* have been.

At 8:00 a.m., more than fourteen hours after the sinking, those dismayed eyes were blessed with, what must have been, a sight sent from Above. There, in the restless, watery distance, was a small, square bump of land! High Island, they would learn later. The haggard sailors riveted their now-alert eyes on the Godsend, carefully, yet suspiciously, watching it grow larger.

The cloud-choked sky was breaking up, reluctantly revealing a once-lost, resplendent sun, which kissed the two men with a searchlight-like glow. With squinting, puffy eyes, the pair carefully regarded each other. Their faces were unnaturally raw, reddened, and swollen, their lips an uncharacteristic bluish-white. Painfully, slowly, Fleming rose to battered, bloodied knees to take a bearing of the land. Elmer hoped it wasn't a mirage. He cautiously looked around, half-expecting another disappointment. But the witch was gone. Fleming concluded the island was real – no – a miracle!

Calculating the drift of the rolling waves, the first mate estimated they would reach the island in a couple of hours. But the men didn't mind the wait; they had all the time in the world.

As he regarded the island, Fleming alarmingly pondered something else. He suddenly wondered if they could survive on land. The water and waves weren't problems anymore. But could they survive on land? Hell, they could reach the island, only to starve to death. Worse, they might never be found, even if there was abundant food.

Could we survive there? Or would the nightmare continue and result in painful death? The questions remained unanswered. The men heard a distant commotion. They looked around. A weathered rescue ship was bearing down on them! Quickly, the sailors were plucked from the lake. For Fleming and Mays, who had experienced a fourteen-and-a-half hour, storm-tossed nightmare that seemed to transcend reality, it was a feeling of indescribable relief. Do you believe in miracles?

(Author's Note: At 4:00 a.m. on November 19, Sundew

Captain Harold Muth told Corpsman Warren Toussaint to get some rest; his services would probably be needed when dawn broke. The corpsman loosely tied himself to a bunk. Awakened by a crew member, Toussaint was informed a raft had been sighted, so he ran out to the buoy deck. He noted the Bradley's *forward raft, about five hundred feet off the* Sundew's *port bow.*

As Captain Muth maneuvered his ship alongside the raft holding Elmer Fleming and Frank Mays, a cargo net was lowered over the side. A Boatswain's mate went down the net to assist the two Bradley *survivors. Fleming and Mays were wrapped in blankets, placed on stretchers and taken to warm quarters, where they could be attended to. They were also given beef broth by Toussaint.)*

On the morning of November 19, at 8:55 a.m., the Coast Guard cutter *Sundew* relayed a wondrous message to the Charlevoix Coast Guard station: "Picked up two survivors on a raft, seventy-one degrees, 5.25 miles from Gull Island." The rescue location was nearly twenty miles from the *Bradley's* grave. The survivors were identified as Elmer Fleming, first mate, and Frank Mays, deck watchman. Both were from Rogers City.

Although physically drained, mentally exhausted and emotionally spent, Fleming and Mays showed concern for fellow crewmen by requesting permission to remain aboard the cutter as it continued search patterns. The request was granted; it seemed beyond human endurance anyone could have survived such a night. "They had a little help. *Someone* looked after them," *Sundew* skipper Harold Muth offered.

In Rogers City the once-guarded hope now was tempered with joy! Two survivors were found so far! The families of Frank Mays and Elmer Fleming rejoiced at their newfound happiness. Others were offered encouraging hope! Telephones remained busy. And prayers continued. Had the Grace of God finally come?

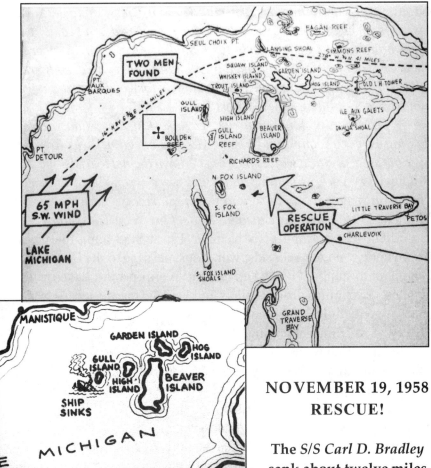

NOVEMBER 19, 1958 RESCUE!

The *S/S Carl D. Bradley* sank about twelve miles southwest of Gull Island, (U.S. Coast Guard map). Elmer Fleming and Frank Mays were found about 5.25 miles northeast of Gull Island. The inset map shows a somewhat exaggerated view. (*Author's Note: The* Edmund Fitzgerald *was launched the year the* Bradley *sank.*)

 Bradley shipwreck

~~~~~ ☐ ~~~~~

CHAPTER 12

" a time to keep silence . . ."
(*Ecclesiastes, 3:7*)

Tired search parties were invigorated. Two survivors were found! What a refreshing relief! If two had managed to survive the storm, then others surely would be rescued! But never judge a book by its cover or a lake by its waves. Jubilant optimism was fleeting, as the shadow of death hovered. A coast guard helicopter reported a gruesome sight. Three bodies were seen floating face-down, one-quarter mile north of Gull Island. Within minutes the number had risen to eight. The search vigil continued.

In the afternoon, the captain of the German vessel *Transontario*, sailing one mile west of High Island, reported he had retrieved a body that had a "breath of life." The cold, shivering sailor was close to death. Yet he was not quite gone. He must have been a helluva swimmer.

"Man may be alive; please rush a doctor!" the German master radioed Charlevoix. Urgent telephone inquiries were made. The nearest doctor was living on Beaver Island, a resort area of some two hundred residents. Dr. Frank E. Luton, 79, learned he would be making an emergency call at sea. A Navy helicopter, piloted by Lt. James Sigman, was rushed to transport the aging physician to the *Transontario*.

The plan was dangerous. Dr. Luton would be lowered to the German vessel's deck via a harness from the hovering helicopter. The helicopter approached the bobbing ship. Dr. Luton was attached to the harness and was clad in a life preserver. He stood ready to be lowered to a windswept deck. Hovering over the ship, the helicopter created a new disturbance on the water as whipping, whining blades cut noisily through the air. Slowly, carefully, surely, the aircraft descended toward a crew-dotted deck. *Just a . . . bit more . . . there!*

The helicopter's doorway opened, and Dr. Luton, whipped by turbulence, stood ready to be lowered. Suddenly a radio message came in; Lt. Sigman talked energetically. He motioned the crew. Dr. Luton stepped back; the door slid shut. Gary Strzelecki was dead of shock and exposure. Dr. Luton sadly returned home. But he endured. Death was no stranger to him.

The Coast Guard search was revealing an ugly trend. By 4:45 p.m., eighteen bodies had been recovered from the cold water. All were clad in now-familiar, orange-colored life jackets. The victims were recovered by various search vessels. Eight were aboard the *Sundew*. The *Hollyhock* reported recovering five lifeless crewmen, while the *Transontario* sailed for Milwaukee with its lone victim. A Beaver Island patrol boat retrieved four bodies found in shoal water. The long search continued for missing crewmen as the afternoon slowly, reluctantly surrendered to darkness.

(*Author's Note: All crewmen reported to have been on watch in the engine room were among those missing. Of the eighteen bodies recovered, eight were the forward-end crew, and ten were the after-end crew.*)

The *Sundew* approached Charlevoix with its grim findings and two survivors. "Babe," a black and white mongrel mascot, was first off the ship. His brisk scampering belied the purpose of the vessel's arrival. The cutter appeared water logged as a wind-shredded flag fluttered uncertainly in the evening air. Tony Spina, ace photographer of the *Detroit Free Press*, was there with his omnipresent camera. *Click. Click. Click.* Spina recorded painful history.

In a strange, ironic twist, before the eight dead men could be removed from the *Sundew*, eleven Coast Guardsmen first had to shove aside the eight-by-ten-foot orange-colored raft that had spared Fleming and Mays. The flat, wooden platform, resting on barrel-like pontoons, sat silently on deck, as if maintaining an honor guard watch over the tarpaulin-covered row of bodies lying next to its battered frame. Dr. Lawrence E. Grate, Robert Winchester and Harold Briggs supervised the transfer of the dead. Most victims were lying on stretchers, covered with olive-green Coast Guard blankets or waterproof tarpaulins. The *Detroit Free Press* photographer clicked.

The *Bradley's* forward raft which saved Fleming and Mays. The men were tossed for more than fourteen hours on raging Lake Michigan waves, floating without direction because the raft's sea anchor had parted.
(*Calcite Screenings*)

(Author's Note: The raft was delivered to the Calcite plant in Rogers City. Today its whereabouts is unknown.)

Cars from Rogers City, Posen, Charlevoix, Cheboygan, St. Ignace and Onaway lined a wind-weary beach as onlookers sadly, silently, somberly, watched the cutter yield its grim findings. Aghast, the crowd cringed as the orange life preserver and arms of a victim could be seen, as it was carried from the ship on a Stokes litter.

(Author's Note: A number of cars along the Charlevoix beach shined their headlights out over Lake Michigan, hoping to spot survivors.)

By 8:35 p.m., seventeen recovered victims had been brought to Charlevoix. The dead were taken to Community Hall across from a funeral home. Earlier in the week the hall was the scene of meetings, a dance, and gala socials. A despondent, gloomy air had supplanted once-cheery surroundings. Now it was a "morgue." Blinds were drawn. Windows were covered with paper.

Michigan Limestone officials made tentative identifications. They telephoned their offices in Rogers City. There, other company men went to waiting families to relate dreaded news. Many offered to drive 'next of kin' to Charlevoix. Some were afraid to make the drive. Hence brothers, uncles and brothers-in-law made the long trip to Charlevoix.

At the locked main door of Community Hall stood Ralph Przybyla of Rogers City. His firm knock was cautiously answered by Police Chief Joseph Smith, a graying, fatherly man.

"I am here to identify Alva Budnick," Ralph said somberly. Budnick was his brother-in-law. Smith led Ralph past the motionless row. They paused at the man believed to be Budnick. The olive-green blanket was pulled down. Ralph only was able to nod. Other identifications followed. Life was continuing.

News reporters interviewed a tired Harold Muth, an 18-year coast guard veteran. What were rescue conditions? "The wind was fifty-five to sixty-five-miles per hour. There were gusts to seventy-five – hurricane. Waves twenty-five to thirty feet," Muth related. "The *Sundew* was rolling fifty degrees to starboard. The deck railing was under water." During the twenty-two hours the *Sundew* was on the water, there was no hot food. The ship was pitching so wildly that pots couldn't be kept on the stove. Coffee was finally manageable.

The bridge was sealed. Gas bottles broke loose and were lost over the side. Every can of paint in the forward locker burst. Paint was sloshing two feet deep in the locker. Many crewmen tied themselves to mess tables to prevent injury. With the ship rolling over fifty degrees, water sprayed down the ship's stack, causing sputtering in the main electrical board in the engine room.
(Conditions aboard the *Sundew*, November 18, 1958)

Although the atmosphere was pervasively negative, Muth offered some hope for the families of the fifteen missing crewmen. "Survival depends on physical condition, the ability to stand exposure, courage and faith. They'll tell you that a man couldn't have lived in the water of Lake Michigan last night for more than one-and-a-half-hours. I remember when I was on duty in Alaska; two men were pulled out of the water after three-and-a-half hours. They lived, and that water's colder than our lake. Who can say?"

At Charlevoix's four-year-old impressive hospital, Elmer Fleming and Frank Mays were admitted for treatment. Both were suffering from shock and hypothermia. But doctors reported the men were in good shape, considering the length of their ordeal. "It's an amazing piece of physical endurance," one of the physicians commented.

A thorough medical examination followed. Then the tired sailors were allowed to rest; later they enjoyed a joyful reunion with their families. Afterwards, the men were asked to share their experiences with reporters. Fleming related, "I was whipped to the bone on that raft. Fighting on those slats all night is no bargain. You can scrape the meat right off your legs trying to get back on the raft, and you don't even feel it (then)."

> **"I've never been so cold in my life. The ice was forming on my jacket and in my hair. But I never stopped praying."**
> – Frank Mays, 26, *Bradley* Deckwatch
>
> **"I didn't want to see how long it was 'til dawn. I was afraid that all the hours that must have passed were maybe only minutes."**
> – Elmer Fleming, 43, *Bradley* First Mate
> (glad he could not see his watch) 11-18-1958
>
> *(Author's Note: Mays and Fleming's reaction to questions posed by the* Detroit Times, *the paper that started the Ship Disaster Fund.)*

Newsmen then asked the pair their thoughts about a rescue. Mays said he believed a rescue was possible if they could somehow make it to daylight. Fleming, too, was confident of a rescue. "Yes -- we're steamboat men. We know how slow it is (how long it takes).

You aren't driving a car around the block out there, but when she came close, that *Sundew* looked big." Later the men were asked if they said any special prayers while they fought for survival.

Mays, a Roman Catholic, replied, "Oh, sure, all of those ("Our Father," "Hail, Mary," Apostle's Creed"), but another one in particular. It's from the Gospel–'Ask in my Father's name, and you shall receive.' Christ said it. I don't know where or who he was talking to, but out there on the raft I used that prayer. I asked and I received."

The crashing Lake Michigan waves could be seen from their clean, warm hospital room as Fleming, a Presbyterian, answered the question more philosophically.

"I couldn't tell you any special prayer. The mysteries of religion are beyond me. You've just got to believe, and that's it. When they say two wives' prayers were answered, what about the other thirty-three? Those other fellows in the water prayed just as hard as us, and their wives prayed all night, just like ours.

"Why my and Frank's prayers were answered is something that we'll never understand. It's like my wife had to tell our son when the report came in that the *Bradley* was sunk. She told him, 'Your father might never come home, Douglas, but you've got to remember, we're not waiting alone'."

November Voices from Rogers City

"It's like those mine disasters we read about. The miners went out Monday morning, and they won't come back. All we can do is wait . . ." "It never happened to us . . . " **"Every time he went away, he was just like a little boy . . . "** "It will be calm where Keith's (Schuler) ship is . . ." **"Almost all the men of the *Bradley*, chums, hunted together, went to school together, like a big family . . . "** "What's needed to tell this story is a phrase, something that a bard might put out like . . . Shakespeare . . ."

"Shakespeare never produced a tragedy greater than that told in the picture of Mrs. Cecelia Krawczak and her six little children, left fatherless on the day her husband was to come home to celebrate her 32nd birthday." — *The Alpena News* (11-20-58)

PORTRAIT OF A TRAGEDY – <u>Top</u>: Cecelia Krawczak, wife of *Bradley* wheelsman Joe Krawczak, holds Jo Lyn, 2 ½ months. Gathered around her are Andrea, 3, Ronald, 11, Jacinta, 10, Kathryn, 4, and Rose Ann, 7... AND A TRIUMPH – Marlys Mays and Mark, 2, and Michael, 4, rejoice at the news of Frank Mays' rescue. <u>Right</u>: The November 20, 1958 edition of the *Presque Isle County Advance*.

Echoing waves . . . and memories

A simple, singular act of nature can trigger a lasting memory – smashing waves in mid-autumn along the beach at our local park. Imagine how cold Lake Michigan is in November.

A brisk forty-mile-per-hour gale may howl at midnight over the majestic white caps of Lake Huron. Imagine a sixty-five-mile-per-hour terror on a witch-like night in November.

A loose shutter on a window may jar your memory into a suddenly vivid past. May remind you of someone you knew when you were younger. Someone who has passed on . . .

My father remembered Paul Heller, a stokerman aboard the *Carl D. Bradley*. He remembers him working as a young man at the A & P Store in Rogers City (when it was located next to the Dime Store on Third Street). He also remembers the night of November 18, 1958, as the worst day in Rogers City's history.

My dad is in his eighties now. Every November 18 he remembers the *Bradley*. And somehow his eyes remain dry. Only the memories cry.

Paul Heller lost his life that fateful November night. And anyone old enough to remember seeing a photo in the *Detroit Times* will tell you they'll never forget the haunting anxiety in the faces of Paul's wife Adeline, and their two children, Raye and Mark.

~~~~ □ ~~~~

CHAPTER 13

"a time to love . . ."
(*Ecclesiastes, 3:8*)

The greenish waves continued rolling, the sands of time. Toiling, swirling movement, whipped by still-restless, homeless winds. The secret was safe.

Eighteen recovered dead. Fifteen missing. A town was cloaked in grief. Waning hope was transformed into cold numbness of tragedy. Twenty-four crewmen called Rogers City "home."

It was a devastating loss, the worst tragedy in the community's history. Those not directly affected by the disaster might have commented, "It wasn't the occurrence of a disaster that was extraordinary; it was the enormity of impact."

On Thursday the town was unusually quiet. Gene Heinzel punctually opened the Brooks Hotel at 8:00 a.m. He attended to some routine chores. Within a few minutes, Gene was slowly drawing a couple of beers for some tired, unshaven deer hunters. There wasn't anyone coming in from "the boats" that day, as they had on Wednesday from the *Cedarville*, a sister ship of the *Bradley*.

Across the street veteran barber Ed Brege stood gazing at Third Street, Rogers City's main street. It wasn't a purposeful gaze. A little boy entered the shop with his mother. Ed was almost startled. He prepared to give the lad a trim. Ed might have moved a little slower this day.

A short distance away Harry Whiteley opened the door of the Advance Publishing Company to begin another business day. He might have searched his memory seeking a time when the community was in such a state of shock. He wouldn't find anything to rival the tragedy. Harry proceeded to put a fresh sheet of paper in his typewriter. The task was heart-wrenching. Not a devastating headline about the sinking. Nor a caption for one of those tragic Shakespearean photos of a victim's family. Instead, Harry began writing obituaries of men he knew.

During the dark day, Rogers City Mayor Ken Vogelheim frantically overworked himself, planning with church ministers for memorial services, while attempting to coordinate the community disaster committee's efforts to assist bereaved families. Then he had to write a memorial proclamation. Funeral director Pete Gatzke opened the forbidding door of his funeral home. He faced a grisly task. Pete had to call in three extra embalmers. Extra caskets would arrive by truck. "We've never handled nine bodies all at once before; we'll have to work all night," he stated grimly. Pete might have to handle even more. Seven coffins stood in the quiet dimness.

Father Adelbert Narloch, a Catholic priest at St. Ignatius Church, consoled those who came to the rectory. During a rare moment of privacy, he examined a list of recovered dead and missing. The check revealed thirteen Catholics. There were already a number of recovered sailors identified as members of his parish. More than five hundred local families professed the Catholic faith. They accounted for nearly half of Rogers City's population. Life, however painful, went on.

The Coast Guard continued a lonely search. It was miraculous and wonderful two survivors were found. But the recovery of eighteen less-fortunate crewmen had created a funereal atmosphere. Yet searchers pressed on. The *Sundew* and *Hollyhock* continued a now-familiar, tedious pattern. Back and forth. Back and forth. More toiling waves, carefully guarding a hideous secret. Many commercial freighters joined the search.

One-hundred-fifty volunteers initiated ground searches of nearby islands. Maybe some crewmen were there, waiting to be rescued! A combing of Gull Island revealed an empty life preserver and considerable debris on the southwest shore. Several life preservers were discovered on the southwest shore of High Island, while a battered, capsized life boat was recovered off the south shore. Subsequent searches of Whiskey, Swan, Squaw and Garden islands proved fruitless. Heavy-hearted searchers went home as darkness claimed the day. The sun rose again.

And the day produced no surprises or miracles. By 4:24 p.m., all units were ordered to discontinue the search upon completion of daylight operations, pending further developments. No trace of the missing. It was as if the lake had swallowed them, refusing to release the men from a watery grave. They were all gone.

Rogers City, Michigan. More negative reports. Sullen reality slowly set in for the waiting families. Time to prepare for the forthcoming emotional trauma. It still seemed like some bad, unreal dream. In less than forty-eight hours, a peaceful community had been transformed into an emotional quagmire. Lifestyles of thousands were being affected.

The town prepared to bury its maritime sons. Thirteen victims were taken to the local high school auditorium. Shocked families and friends paid respects. Two large American flags, between which reposed a large, floral anchor, formed an alcove where the coffins were placed. Mayor Vogelheim proclaimed Saturday as a day of mourning. Flags were ordered at half-staff for thirty days. Business places closed in respect for its lost citizens. Yet the human factor remained strong. Mrs. Betty Sweeney of Bloomfield Township traveled to Rogers City to attend the mass burial rites. Her brother, Alfred Boehmer, was a second assistant engineer on the *Bradley*. She was deeply moved by the stoic courage shown by the townspeople.

"We were received at the funeral home by representatives of the disaster committee, as were scores of kin who had come from out of town. Fifty townspeople turned over their homes to mourners who had come some distance. There were five hundred cars in the funeral procession, and not one of them was driven by a close relative of the deceased. Townspeople drove the cars. Many did not know the drivers by name. People didn't do a whole lot of talking about it. They were just there. They took groups of mourners into their homes and fed them. It was a spontaneous thing that moved us deeply."

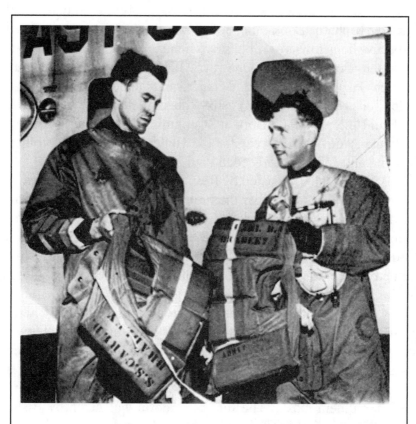

Coast Guard rescuers hold *Bradley* life preservers. The *Bradley* sinking led to new life jacket regulations from the U.S. Coast Guard. Crotch straps were mandated on life jackets, as well as new regulations related to rescue signaling devices.

The *Bradley* sinking was the most severe loss of life on Lake Michigan since the violent gales of November 11, 1940 – the 'Armistice Day Storms.' (*The Alpena News*)

Funeral services were held on Saturday and Sunday. Carl Bartell, Richard Book and John Zoho were returned to their respective hometowns of Kalkaska, Michigan; Portsmouth, Iowa; and Claireton, Pennsylvania. Onaway, Michigan, hometown of brave seamen Gary Price and Cleland Gager, held memorial services for its fallen sons. In Rogers City Pastor Robert Weller held solemn rites for Paul Heller and Paul Horn at St. John Lutheran Church. It was a particularly devastating year for the Heller family. Two brothers, William and John, had preceded Paul in death that year.

Rev. Weller, assisted by Rev. Louis A. Linn, told the widow of seaman Heller not to fear the future "because God in his infinite wisdom provides special care for those remaining after the departure of loved ones." Weller quoted Heller's favorite Bible passage: "If God be for us, who can be against us?" The jam-packed, white-framed church was a place of somber meditation as echoes of "Jesus, Savior, Pilot Me" filtered through the gray, dreary November air.

A mass funeral was held Saturday at St. Ignatius Church. Nearly two thousand mourners attended the Catholic rite. Flower-strewn, flag-draped caskets were slowly carried by sixty pall bearers, under an arch of crossed swords held by twenty-four full-dress Knights of Columbus. Reverend Narloch's echoing voice intoned the solemn requiem mass. The funeral oratorio was given by Bishop Steven Woznicki of Saginaw, Michigan. The atmosphere was one of strained silence. A few, whimpering sobs tugged at the heartstrings of many. An American flag flew at half-staff just outside the church.

Bishop Woznicki conducted the funeral rites, reminding those present that "These men represented the highest examples of fidelity so necessary to our democracy, fidelity to work and fidelity to family." A few more sobs. Flag-draped coffins stood in a neat row. Woznicki's penetrating voice continued.

"God is the master of the elements. Is it possible that in our progress in science, we are getting too proud? While reaching for the stars and moon, we have not yet mastered our elements of air, water and fire." The bishop's strong voice had a visual impact on those he could reach. Others could not hear him, dazed by another world.

Perhaps it was better that way.

Woznicki also reflected, "This tragedy has touched the heartstrings of the State of Michigan. But if we don't watch ourselves in a situation like this, we will become bitter against God. We cannot hope to fathom the reasons for God's actions, but some answers are in the principles of Christianity. We cannot but say, 'thy will be done.'

Two thousand mourners packed St. Ignatius Catholic Church to attend rites for *Bradley* crewmen. There were sixty pall bearers. Burial was at Mt. Calvary Cemetery.
(Presque Isle County Advance)

"The great company for which these men worked, with 400,000 hearts, will not let these people down. I hope the fifty children left behind will remember their fathers as heroes." Mt.

Calvary – the site of Catholic burials. On a windswept hillside, mourners said goodbye as Bob Centala's haunting trumpet rendition of "Taps" echoed into an iron coldness.

"There was a funeral on every street. Rogers City just couldn't hold all the grief . . ."
– Mayor Ken Vogelheim

Under the drawn swords of the Knights of Columbus, pallbearers bear a coffin of a *Bradley* sailor at St. Ignatius Catholic Church in Rogers City. (*The Alpena News*)

The *Carl D. Bradley* was now a ghost of the sea.

As the community was memorializing the dead, the crews of the *Bradley's* sister ships paid tribute to their lost peers. Four ships were docked at Calcite harbor. While restless Lake Huron waves lapped against steel, gray hulls, crewmen attended funeral services in Rogers City. On Saturday, November 22, four Bradley Transportation Line ships "dropped anchor" at noon: the *T.W. Robinson* at Buffalo, New York; the *Rogers City* at Chicago, Illinois; the *Myron C. Taylor* at Conneaut, Ohio; and the *Cedarville* at Port Huron, Michigan.

Separate funeral services were conducted for local crewmen at McWilliams and Gatzke funeral homes. Nationwide prayer services were offered in memory of the lost sailors. With the recovered dead now resting in peace, Rogers City returned to the business of living, although life had become extremely tempered now. Lives were shattered. The pieces were difficult to pick up.

Yet the town was not alone. Messages of sympathy and offers of help poured in from across America: From Chicago, Illinois: "We are shocked and grieved at the disaster which has befallen the *Steamer Bradley* and the people of Rogers City." From Ft. Wayne, Indiana: "We are overcome at the tragedy of the *Bradley*." From Cheboygan, Michigan: "We extend our condolences . . ." From

Congressman Victor Knox: "It is with heartfelt grief . . ." From Marine City, Michigan: "We, as sailors in an understanding community, wish to express . . ."

The feelings of many were well-expressed by the following. "We wish to express and to extend our sympathy to the families of our fellow crewmen, the men of the *Str. Bradley*, who were victims of the tragedy a short time ago. The men of the ships of the Bradley Fleet have always been close, perhaps because of their maritime calling, and perhaps because most of us are closely associated as friends and neighbors. The same friendship that existed between the men of the fleet extends to the families of those who have been lost. We stand ready to be helpful in any way we can in these sad hours."

The message was signed, 'The Crew of the *I. L. Clymer*.' The *Clymer* once bore the name *Carl D. Bradley*.

Relatives and friends offered comfort and help. Some families were concerned about financial security. Their breadwinners were gone; the bereaved faced an uncertain future. All *Bradley* crewmen carried a minimum $3,500 insurance policy with some having as much as $28,000. Members of the Michigan Limestone Disaster Committee helped beneficiaries apply for company life insurance benefits. Officials also assisted families in securing financial aid from a company savings plan to which many of the men had contributed. Some qualified for funds under Michigan Limestone's contributory pension plan, while many sought Social Security benefits. Each widow or family member received $300 for lost personal belongings. Funeral expenses were also reimbursed.

The *Detroit Times* created the Carl D. Bradley Ship Disaster Children's Fund by donating $1,000. The fund, designed to provide financial security for the health, welfare and education of fatherless children, was to be administered by banker John Blasky, Mayor Ken Vogelheim and three local ministers (Adelbert Narloch, Robert Weller, and Frederick Steen).

A sympathetic, understanding nation opened its heart – and its pocket book – to the children. In big gifts and small, many people expressed how deeply they were touched by the tragedy.

~ ~ ~

"I like to make a little help."
Jesus Montoya, a contributor to the
Carl D. Bradley Ship Disaster Children's Fund

~ ~ ~

(Author's Note: The night of November 18, 1958, is quite unlike anything we'd ever seen in this small town. It would have been very easy to get "caught up" in the tragedy of the moment.

The people of Rogers City are generous souls. When disaster strikes, they truly feel the victims' pain. They cook food for grieving families. Run errands at the drop of a hat. Give generously of their time. Find nickels, dimes and quarters to give to needy families.

Those not old enough to have witnessed the generous spirit of Rogers City during the dark days of November 1958 certainly will bear testament to its great heart in February 2008, when five members of a family perished in a tragic house fire.)

When the *Detroit Times* announced its fund-raising campaign, Jesus Montoya, 75, and grandfather of eight, shuffled into the newspaper's hectic office. He couldn't read too well. His income was only $136 per month. Jesus paid $36 monthly for his small room. He slowly walked over to a representative of the fund-raising campaign. "I like to make a little help," he said, as a wrinkled hand extended a ten-dollar bill. Within hours the fund had mushroomed to $13,000.

More than $154,000 would be donated. Eligible children received equal shares of the proceeds. Fund trustees enrolled the children in a group health insurance plan. The trustees, who served without compensation, invested $100,000 in government bonds, while other contributions were put in 3 percent saving certificates. The fund was a nonprofit corporation. Many children would receive a college education through the financial windfall.

There were some financial difficulties. Michigan Limestone officials met with families and offered each a death benefit. A lump sum $660,000 offer was presented, with the condition it be accepted by a sufficient number of families. This would enable the company to proceed with the mechanics of settlement.

However, by the date set for acceptance of the company's offer, officials learned legal representatives of ten families had filed damage suits claiming more than seven million dollars in liability. Consequently, the company withdrew its initial offer. Following years of legal wrangling and red tape, final $1.2 million cash settlements were distributed among the families.

The families were very appreciative of the efforts of the U.S. Coast Guard. The Coast Guard had once again performed admirably under most adverse conditions. Indeed, long after rescue operations were officially terminated, the Coast Guard conducted daily air searches of the area until it became readily apparent that no one else had survived the casualty. (*Author's Note: Aircraft from the Coast Guard Air Station at Traverse City spent 122 hours searching the casualty area from November 18 to December 9.*

The following Coast Guard units participated in the rescue emergency: Plum Island Life Boat Station–dispatched but, due to heavy seas, unable to proceed; Charlevoix Life Boat Station – The commanding officer recalled a small boat due to heavy weather; Beaver Island Moorings – held in readiness but not dispatched to the scene due to heavy weather; the rescue ships already noted.)

The captains of nine commercial ships which participated in search-rescue efforts were mailed letters of commendation from the Coast Guard's Ninth District Commander, Rear Admiral Joseph Kerrins: *"We wish to express our appreciation for the services rendered by you and your crew in the search for survivors of the S/S Carl D. Bradley. In answering the call of distress, you showed courage in diverting your course, in the face of dangerous waters and extremely high seas, in the hope of lending assistance to the crew of the stricken ship. You are to be congratulated upon this fine performance of duty."*

This letter was sent to the following skippers: Walter Zeitlien, *Transontario*; Harold Viksjo, *Sylvania*; J. A. Sykes, *Algocen*; Paul Mueller, *Christian Sartori*; Sven Fagerstrom, *Henry Ford II*; D. E. Nauts, *John G. Munson*; J. B. Sullivan, *Johnstown*; E. M. Magnuson, *Elton Hoytt II*; and J. V. Osier, *Robert C. Stanley*.

Captains of the Bradley fleet bring Christmas joy to the children of the *Bradley* crewmen. Left to right: Captain Donald Nauts (S/S *John G. Munson*) holds Eric Boehmer, 9 months;

Captain William Chain (S/S *Myron C. Taylor*), with Susan Greengtski, 8 months; Captain Donald Monroe (S/S *Calcite*) with Andrea Krawczak, 3; Captain Oscar Miller (S/S *Cedarville*) and Kim Budnick, 3; Captain Alex Malocha (S/S *I. L. Clymer*) holds Toni Budnick, 2. (*Calcite Screenings*)

"I remember the water color paints . . ."

Brenda (Kowalski) Lamp was only eight years old when she lost her father, Raymond Joseph Kowalski, on the *Bradley*. She was at her grandparents' home (Benjamin and LaVerne Strzelecki) when news of the sinking reached Rogers City.

"When it happened, I remember being 'shuttled' to Bud and Connie Jackson's house. They were our next-door neighbors. I was given water colors to paint with."

Brenda married Malcolm "Mac" Lamp, who lost his father on the *Cedarville*. Like his father and grandfather, "Mac" is a chief engineer. He presently sails on the *Buffalo*. Brenda and "Mac" have two sons, Shaun and Erik.

Today Brenda Lamp, whose uncle was Gary Strzelecki, teaches at Rogers City Elementary School.

. . . and Rogers City remembers the *Carl D. Bradley*.

(Calcite Screenings)

Neptune's Dusk

Distorted steel now
settled deep shows
whiter shades of gray,

Your pilot house sits
silent still, no longer
greets the day,

Intrepid depths of misty storms along life's sandy stream,
A sepulcher in Neptune's dusk, time transforms the dream
– James L. Hopp

(Top: *Calcite Screenings/* Above: *Mayday! Mayday!*
Kenneth E. Friedrich [Reverse]

CHAPTER 14

"and a time of peace . . ."
(Ecclesiastes, 3:8)

Thirty-five seafaring men. A giant, proud steamer. An angry November storm. A deathly specter. The single, most important question concerning the sinking of the *Bradley* will be debated for generations. What caused the massive steamer to be swallowed by a violent, frenzied gale? There was speculation. Questioned judgement. Theories about the carrier's rapid plunge to the dark, murky depths of Lake Michigan.

Forrest Pearse, who had captained the *Bradley* for sixteen years, wondered whether "metal fatigue," coupled with the effect of a tidal wave, might have caused the ship's untimely end. "The ship might have been caught on two huge waves, with the midships just hanging in the air," Pearse opinionated. "That could have caused the breakup."

Others would point to letters written by Captain Roland Bryan, who seemed to indicate the *Bradley* was less-than-seaworthy. In a letter written November 8, 1958, to Mrs. Florence Herd of Port Huron, Bryan wrote, "This boat is getting pretty ripe for too much weather . . . I'll be glad when they get her fixed up . . . It's been a screwy season all the way through . . . "

Similar concern was voiced in Bryan's letter to a friend, Ken Faweet, when the *Bradley* captain lamented, "The hull is not good -- have to nurse her along . . . 'take it easy' were my instructions . . . the hull was badly damaged at Cedarville . . ."

There was uneasiness, voiced by a deck watchman and first assistant engineer, that the great vessel should have been dry docked for repairs. They were concerned that the bulkheads were rusted so badly one could see from one compartment to the next, that the ship had rust pouring from its holds on trips prior to the fatal run, that the ballast tanks leaked constantly, that the pumps had to be kept on full-time to carry off water in the cargo hold, and that – at times – there was as much as one foot of water in the tunnel.

U.S. Steel Corporation officials argued the *Bradley* was certified as "seaworthy" by the Coast Guard. That the great vessel had been subjected to a higher-than-average Coast Guard inspection process to ensure a high level of safety. The company stated the limestone carrier had dry docked no less than eighteen times in its thirty-one-year history, in contrast to the six mandated dry docks for sight-and-survey inspections of the hull. As recently as June, 1957, the steamer had undergone a shipyard inspection.

(*Author's Note: The* Bradley *was also in dry dock from May 9-15 at Chicago, Illinois, to complete repairs incident to damages sustained on April 3, 1956, in a collision with the M/V* White Rose *at South East Bend, St. Clair River. The* Bradley *sustained damage near its #10 hatch on the starboard side. These repairs consisted of inserting one new bilge plate (twenty-one feet long) to replace the damaged sections of plates on the starboard side, and minor fairing and riveting of two shell plates on the port side.)*

Company spokesmen also cited the National Safety Council's recognition of the fleet's time-honored safety procedures. A few officials intimated the *Bradley* may have struck a "doom pinnacle"– some uncharted rocks or reef – which may have contributed to the sinking. This theory was later discounted when the 150-foot vessel *Williams* surveyed the wreckage site and found no such hazard existed in the area where the *Bradley* sank.

(*Author's Note: The opinion of the United States Coast Guard's Board of Inquiry found that the* Bradley *did not strike Boulder Reef, as some have suggested. Had the vessel struck Boulder Reef, the Board stated, both parts of the hulk, by reason of their dimensions, would be visible in the water of less than a 60-foot depth, which extends for a distance of about three miles northeast of the reef, along the track the* Carl D. Bradley *would have made.*

On June 23, 1942, the Eugene J. Buffington *struck Boulder Reef and later sank. She was raised twenty-five days later and taken to Harbor Springs, MI, and then to the American Ship Building Company at South Chicago, IL, for repairs.*)

Other theorists speculated the very construction of the vessel might have caused it to become structurally weakened by the constant battering of waves. The violent action of the storm may have caused a certain number of rivets to shear off from the hull. The rivets held the ship's steel plates together. Modern steamships have their plates welded, but when older ships docked after a major blow, there were always rivet heads to be picked up in the holds.

Many marine engineers verify this, claiming rivet heads can be picked up by the bucketful. And anyone who has been alongside a freighter during rough weather has experienced the uncanny phenomenon of being pelted with rivets; they break off from the steel hull plates and shoot out like bullets from a gun.

"The first time I was on her, I'd say to the watchman, 'What's all that noise (ping!-ping!)?' He said, 'Ah, the rivets poppin' out of the side tanks.'" –Leonard Gabrysiak

"When you stood on the bow and looked back, you could not see the stern of the ship."
– Kenneth E. Friedrich, describing the *Bradley* in a rolling sea

As in all marine-related disasters, the U.S. Coast Guard Commandant Alfred C. Richmond ordered a full investigation of the sinking. A four-man board of inquiry, headed by Rear Admiral Joseph Kerrins, went to Rogers City to secure testimony from survivors, company officials and the Coast Guard. Commanders Charles Leising and Joseph Change also were on the board, as was Lt. Commander Garth H. Read.

Following months of exhaustive, intensive testimony, the

Coast Guard issued its long-awaited findings. The board of inquiry suggested the *Bradley* might have developed some "undetected structural weakness or defect," which ultimately resulted in its sinking. The report also charged Captain Bryan with exercising "poor judgement" in attempting to cross the storm-battered reaches of northern Lake Michigan. Commandant Richmond reviewed the board's findings. He disapproved of the conclusions.

Richmond maintained the *Bradley's* structural weaknesses were *not* undetected because unexplained hairline cracks were discovered in the vessel's hull while it was dry docked in Chicago in 1957. (*Author's Note: Some of these cracks were up to six feet long.*)

The Coast Guard commandant also stated that two groundings of the carrier went unreported to the Coast Guard. The groundings occurred at Cedarville, Michigan (one in the spring and one in November of 1958). Richmond noted the second grounding incident resulted in a 14-inch keel fracture, which was subsequently repaired.

(*Author's Note: The U.S. Coast Guard's final report suggested the following concerning life jackets/lifeboats. Main points: (1)* **"That a jacket-type life preserver be provided** *with a crotch strap to hold the jacket down on the body and with a collar to support the head out of the water." (2)* **"That a second, additional life raft or other approved buoyant apparatus be mandatory** *for all Great Lakes' cargo vessels of three hundred gross tons and over with one raft in the forward part of the vessel and one in the after-end." (3)* **"That each lifeboat on all Great Lakes' cargo vessels of over three thousand tons be fitted** *with mechanical disengaging apparatus." (4)* **"That each lifeboat and life raft on all Great Lakes' cargo vessels be provided** *with at least six red parachute-type flare distress signals and the means to project them."*)

Courts and historians would have to weigh all the theories and testimony. The two survivors indicated there was little advance warning the ship was in serious trouble. A positive identification of the sunken steamer has been made via an underwater television camera. The survey revealed the vessel is lying in 360 feet of water.

Insured by Lloyds of London for $8,000,000, the *Bradley* has been judged unsalvageable. Even if salvageable, the two thousand tons of the *Bradley's* usable scrap metal would bring in no more than $80,000 at the mill, one-tenth the amount the company had planned to spend on a cargo hold at the end of the '58 season.

Many words have been written describing the sinking of the *Bradley*. Perhaps author William Ratigan put it best. "The greatest shipwreck in modern annals of the Great Lakes had happened in one thunderbolt moment off storm-washed Gull Island and Boulder Reef in the Beavers; the largest ship ever to go down in Great Lakes history had plummeted to the bottom of the northern reaches of the third largest body of fresh water in America; and thirty-three men, with all their hopes and dreams, were lost in Lake Michigan."

We may never know what exactly happened that fateful November day. Perhaps an act of God decided to call the sailors to some destiny mere mortals cannot fathom. Many times we look out at the water and remember. Gentle winds and lazy, rolling waves belie the true character of the water. The lake, as ever, contains a myriad of ghosts. But the naive are unable to sense them.

Christmas soon arrived in Rogers City. Yet many were burdened with bleak hopes. But it wasn't total despair. Gifts of toys, food and clothing rolled in by the truckload. Mrs. Melville Orr, a widow, commented, "Most of the youngsters probably had a bigger Christmas than they ever had in their lives."

Toni Budnick, 2, got a toy chicken while Melvin (Gary) Orr, 10, fired his toy machine gun. Michael Kowalski, 6, pushed an army toy truck across carpeting while Kathryn Krawczak, 4, received a new doll. Tiny Posen, the "potato capital of the world," sent two huge baskets, including turkey with all the trimmings, to each family.

And families would remember the kindness. Would remember the memorials. The *Presque Isle County Advance*, in one of its most unforgettable publications, memorialized the disaster in its November 27, 1958, edition. The newspaper carried extensive coverage of the tragedy, including a special photo section. One of the most haunting photographs can be found on page four. It showed a lone limestone carrier docked next to an empty berth where the *Bradley* was to have been tied up. The long, gray ship in the photo was the *Cedarville*.

Like the American soldier who died in battle, the *Bradley* crew would be remembered on Memorial Day.

Rogers City would survive the devastating shock although part of it died that bleak November night.

Emotionally and psychologically, the small community had suffered some deep wounds that time would partially heal. At the end of 1958, Rogers City, like America, had experienced profound change.

Never again would the *S/S Carl D. Bradley* dock next to her sister ship, the *S/S Cedarville*, shown here at Calcite.
(*Presque Isle County Advance*)

Life Goes On
by Sheri Bruder

Their only hope was to wait till dawn,
As they struggled alone cuz their friends were gone,
They sailed with pride that very same day,
Now they lived their lives to see the sun's rays,
They clung to the raft and they prayed like hell,
And death grew closer each time they fell,
Two were gone and two remained,
The water wanted them but they restrained,
The witch enclosed them as their hands became numb,
And to the raft the two men clung,
The fateful day is remembered sadly
By the only survivors of the *Carl D. Bradley*
(*Calcite Screenings*)

Karma

by Sarah Stringer

Underwater, still, silent. Many years ago, we have spared. It is a graveyard now, resembling Atlantis. Can you remember? . . . That shadow of death with burning red eyes, reaching out, grasping for our souls, no white immaculate lights, no angels, just despair, and loud laughter of gods and devils . . .

While we clinched our imaginary crosses close to our hearts . . . Oh, the lives that flashed before our eyes! We hoped for our Lord to save us! . . . Never again will it be so, now, that we shall go to heaven. What heaven? Why heaven? When heaven? Where is that heaven? This heaven, oh earth . . . Or shall it be called everlasting life? . . . Silence, but only for our mortal bodies . . . Rebirth, our old souls carry on. Karma.

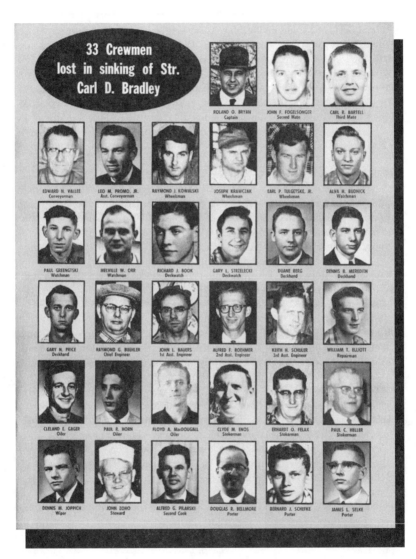

33 Crewmen lost in sinking of Str. Carl D. Bradley

ROLAND O. BRYAN
Captain

JOHN F. FOGELSONGER
Second Mate

CARL R. BARTELL
Third Mate

EDWARD N. VALLEE
Conveyorman

LEO M. PROMO, JR.
Asst. Conveyorman

RAYMOND J. KOWALSKI
Wheelsman

JOSEPH KRAWCZAK
Wheelsman

EARL P. TULGETSKE, JR.
Wheelsman

ALVA H. BUDNICK
Watchman

PAUL GREENGTSKI
Watchman

MELVILLE W. ORR
Watchman

RICHARD J. BOOK
Deckwatch

GARY L. STRZELECKI
Deckwatch

DUANE BERG
Deckhand

DENNIS B. MEREDITH
Deckhand

GARY N. PRICE
Deckhand

RAYMOND G. BUEHLER
Chief Engineer

JOHN L. BAUERS
1st Asst. Engineer

ALFRED F. ROEHMER
2nd Asst. Engineer

KEITH H. SCHULER
3rd Asst. Engineer

WILLIAM T. ELLIOTT
Repairman

CLELAND E. GAGER
Oiler

PAUL R. HORN
Oiler

FLOYD A. MacDOUGALL
Oiler

CLYDE M. ENOS
Stokerman

ERHARDT O. FELAX
Stokerman

PAUL C. HELLER
Stokerman

DENNIS M. JOPPICH
Wiper

JOHN ZOHO
Steward

ALFRED G. PILARSKI
Second Cook

DOUGLAS R. BELLMORE
Porter

BERNARD J. SCHEFKE
Porter

JAMES L. SELKE
Porter

+ Roland Bryan, 52, Loudonville, New York, Single;   + John Fogelsonger, 31, St. Ignace, Michigan (Wife - Mary, Children - Deborah, 5, Infant, 1 Month)   # Carl Bartell, 25, Kalkaska, Michigan (Wife - Joan, Children - Carla, 3)   # Edward Vallee, 49, Rogers City (Wife - Frances, Children - Barry, 22, Patricia, 15, Sue, 12)   # Leo Promo, Jr., 21, Rogers City (Wife - Mary)   # Raymond Kowalski, 31, Rogers City (Wife - Mavis, Children - Brenda, 8, Michael, 6, Richard, 2)   # Joseph Krawczak, 35, Rogers City (Wife - Cecelia, Children - Ronald, 11, Jacinta, 10, Rose, 7, Kathryn, 4, Andrea, 3, Jo Lynn, 2 ½ Months)

+ Earl Tulgetske, 30, Rogers City (Wife - Eleanore, Children - Karen, 6, Susan, 5, Paul, 3, Leslie, 14 months,   # Alva Budnick, 26, Rogers City (Wife - Frances, Children - Kim, 3, Toni, 2)   +Paul Greengtski, 23, Rogers City (Wife -Patricia, Children - Susan, 7 Months)   + Melville Orr, 35, Rogers City (Wife - Barbara, Children - Susan, 12, Patti, 11, Melvin (Gary), 10)   # Richard Book , 26, Portsmouth, Iowa, Single   # Gary Strzelecki, 21, Rogers City (Wife - Ann, Children - Benjamin, 9 Months)   + Duane Berg, 25, Rogers City (Wife - Donna)   + Dennis Meredith, 25, Metz, Michigan, Single   # Gary Price, 21, Onaway, Michigan (Wife - Helen, Children - Ronald, 4 Months)

+ Raymond Buehler, 59, Lakewood, Ohio (Wife - Francis, Children - Bonnita Ann, 19)   + John Bauers, 30, Rogers City (Wife - Aileen, Children - Mark, 3, Jerry, 1) # Alfred Boehmer, 32, Rogers City, (Wife - Dolores, Children - Phillip, 2, Eric, 8 Months)

+ Keith Schuler, 36, Rogers City (Wife -Marjorie, Children - Duwayne, 15, Randy, 11, Jane, 6)   # William Elliot, 26, Rogers City, (Wife - Sandra, Children - William, 3 Months)   # Cleland Gager, 30, Onaway Michigan, (Wife -Patricia, Children - Cheryl, 8, Michael, 6, Daniel, 4)   # Paul Horn, 21, Rogers City, Single

+ Floyd MacDougall, 26, Rogers City (Wife - Genevieve Children - Debra, 4, Denise, 6 Months)   + Martin Enos, 29, Cheboygan Michigan, Single   # Erhardt Felax, 46, Rogers City (Wife -Barbara, Children - Linda, 11, Donna, 7)   # Paul Heller, 45, Rogers City (Wife - Adeline, Children - Mark,17, Raye, 12)

+ Dennis Joppich, 19, Rogers City, Single   # John Zoho, 63, Claireton, Pennsylvania, Single   # Alfred Pilarski, 30, Rogers City, Single   + Douglas Bellmore, 34, Onaway, Michigan (Wife - Flora, Children-Linda, 11, Sharon, 9, Terry, 5)

Bernard Schefke, 18, Rogers City, Single   + James Selke, 18, Rogers City, Single

Survivors: Elmer Fleming, 43, Rogers City, (Wife - Mary, Children - Douglas ,15)
Frank Mays, 26, Rogers City, (Wife - Marlys, Children - Michael, 4, Mark, 2, Frank, 1 Month)

+ **Missing**   # Recovered   Average Age: 31.5 Years

PRAY FOR THE SOULS OF

ERHARDT FELAX
ALFRED BOEHMER
ALVA BUDNICK
LEO PROMO, JR.
ALFRED PILARSKI
BERNARD SCHEFKE
JOSEPH KRAWCZAK
WILLIAM ELLIOTT

PASSED AWAY
November 18, 1958
after sinking of
The Str. Carl D. Bradley

PRAYER

O God, the Creator and Redeemer of all the faithful, grant unto the souls of Thy servants departed the remission of all their sins; that, by pious supplication, they may obtain that pardon which they have always desired. Grant this, O God, Who livest and reignest forever and ever.

Amen.

Gatzke Funeral Home
Rogers City

In 1959 Captain Donald Nauts and crew searched the area near Boulder Reef for the *Carl D. Bradley* shipwreck. Nauts used a Sea Scanner, a sonar device, to explore Lake Michigan's bottom for unusual sound waves. They discovered what they believed to be the *Bradley*. According to the sonar device, the *Bradley* was in 360 feet of water and in one piece, contradicting Elmer Fleming's and Frank Mays' testimony, as well as the conclusions of the U. S. Coast Guard report.

The Bradley Transportation Company wanted to confirm Nauts' findings, so it brought in the *Submarex,* a 175-foot underwater search ship. The *Submarex* was equipped with an underwater television camera. The exploration team spent ten days over the target, concluding it was the wreck of the *Bradley*.

Michigan Limestone Company President Christian Beukema said the television camera confirmed the *Bradley* was in one piece, just as earlier sonar findings had indicated. The company did state, however, that there were breaks in the *Bradley's* deck. Beukema also said the *Submarex* saw either a full name or portion of the name *Carl D. Bradley*. Bradley Transportation officials also claimed to have photographs showing the ship in one piece, rather than two.

"The so-called pictures that U.S. Steel had taken, saying the ship was in one piece, were never produced. I've never seen them." – Frank Mays

"I don't know whatever happened to them (the pictures). The New York Admiralty Council had them, and they were probably destroyed. The case was over." – Christian Beukema

"Chris Beukema was not on the *Bradley* the night she sank. I was there; I saw the ship break in two," Mays said.

In August 1995, Bernie Hellstrom, an electrical contractor and diver, and his son Andy relocated the wreck of the *Bradley*. Using a drop-down, black-and-white video camera he had designed himself, Hellstrom filmed sections of the ship. His video revealed fuzzy images: a port hole, the stern house, and a companionway.

Also in 1995, video images of the *Bradley* were captured during the DeepQuest Expedition, led by Fred Shannon. Bernie Hellstrom accompanied the expedition and verified the position of the *Bradley* with his drop camera. *Bradley* survivor Frank Mays was brought along on this expedition as well. For years Mays insisted the *Bradley* broke in two during the violent Lake Michigan storm. U.S. Steel adamantly maintained Mays was mistaken, that the ship was in one piece.

The DeepQuest Expedition in 1995 featured the 5,000-pound *Delta* submersible. The *Delta* is a two-man submersible with a three-day air supply. The pilot sits and navigates the submersible while the passenger must lie on the floor and look out one of its circular ports. The *Delta* is also equipped with a three-pronged grappling claw. It typically travels from 1-3 knots.

The first two days of the DeepQuest Expedition '95 were hampered by poor weather and visibility. The *Bradley* lies in an area where heavy silt can be kicked up by Lake Michigan's currents. On the third day of the expedition, however, *Delta* pilot David Slater, accompanied by *Bradley* survivor Frank Mays, saw the name plate on the *Bradley's* hull, positively identifying the wreck.

Mays noted the red paint he had used to paint the ship's railing only a few days before the disaster. Attached to the *Delta's* grappling arm was a plaque honoring the lost crew of the *Carl D. Bradley*. The plaque was dropped on the *Bradley's* deck.

"I was there."
– Frank Mays, upon returning
from his dive to the *Carl D. Bradley*
aboard the *Delta* submersible

(Author's Note: The two-man Delta *sub was for lease and was in constant use around the world. It had been used for diving on oil drilling sites, doing surveys of marine life, and exploring earthquake faults of the U.S. Pacific Coast. The* Bradley *dive was the 3,687th for the* Delta.*)*

Two years later, the Expedition '97 team, with Shannon, Mays, Hellstrom and artist James Clary, returned to the shipwreck site. The lengthy documentation took twenty-six hours. Film footage revealed the *Bradley* lying at a depth ranging from 320 to 380 feet. The search team claimed there is an approximately ninety-foot gulf between the forward and aft sections. The aft port corner of the forward section seemed to have struck Lake Michigan's bottom first. The bow is in near-perfect condition, with depth markings readable to the lowest point. Lake Michigan's strong, swirling currents have washed away the lake's bottom under the *Bradley*, leaving a five to six-foot space beneath the bow. There is a visible stress crack on the port-side hull.

Frank Mays recalls the fateful night of November 18, 1958. (Mike Modrzynski)

There are also murky images of a port-side pilot house door and the *Bradley's* bell. The *Bradley's* long unloading boom still rests in its cradle; the boom is secured by its stays. Parts of the ship are strewn nearby: the steering pole, forward mast, radar and main mast. The stern is lying at an approximate forty-degree angle; the propeller and rudder are off the lake bottom. Many hatch covers are missing, and some rail stanchions are gone, hanging out of position or severely bent. There is a tremendous amount of coal scattered around the ship, and the pilot house window glass is missing.

Elmer Fleming, who broadcast the *Bradley's* Mayday call, would have been surprised to learn that the microphone's cord is still visible in the pilot house, stretched across the lower portion of a port pilot house window. The ship's steering wheel is also visible. "The *Carl D. Bradley* lies upright on the bottom in two separate pieces," Frank Mays said.

Fred Shannon (left) and Frank Mays explored the *Bradley* shipwreck in 1995 and 1997. Poor weather and visibility hampered the '95 expedition. Expedition '97 yielded more positive results. (Expedition '97)

Much is made of the sinking of the *Edmund Fitzgerald* on Lake Superior on November 10, 1975. Gordon Lightfoot's romanticized (and not always accurate) song has made it one of the most discussed shipwrecks. The *Bradley* became the "ship that time forgot," despite having lost more crewmen (33) than the *Fitzgerald* (29). In recent years, however, interest in the *Bradley* sinking has increased. **October 11, 1998:** Explorer Steve Libert was searching for an aircraft which had disappeared over Lake Michigan. But what he discovered with his video-drop camera was something unexpected – the hulk of something large. The black-and-white images, reminiscent of Bernie Hellstrom's, showed some deck railings. Libert checked positions and depth, confirming he had stumbled upon the *Carl D. Bradley*.

August 7, 2001: Mirek Standowicz became the first diver ever to visit the wreck of the *Carl D. Bradley*. Standowicz, with help from Jim and Pat Stayer, released the first excellent video record of the *Bradley* at the bottom of Lake Michigan: pilot house views, lower level cabins, parts of the ship's unloading boom. The video corroborated what Expedition '97 had learned: the *Bradley* is in a very preserved state, with paint still visible.

July 2004: Greg Such of the Shipwrecking Adventures group, along with John Scoles and John Janzen, headed for the *Bradley's* resting place. Diving from the support ship *Little Alexandria,* the team became the first to reach the *Bradley's* stern. The divers also explored the ship's bow and pilot house. Roughly a half-hour of video footage was taken, and one of the photographs released shows a view from slightly below the stern. BRADLEY and, under that, NEW YORK, are clearly visible.

July 23, 2004: Captain Bill Prince took his *M/V Nordic Diver* and seven divers to the wreck. Divers toured the pilot house and bow for two days; camera problems prevented divers from photographing the wreck. **July 21-23, 2005**: Greg Such returned to the site; Frank Mays was present for at least one day of the dives. Visibility was excellent; the photographs revealed how well Lake Michigan's cold waters have preserved the *Bradley.* John Janzen, along with three other divers, landed near the after-end of the unloading boom's A-frame. They took photographs of the upward slant of the boom's cables and the shape of the boom.

August 7, 2007: Professional divers John Janzen and John Scoles of Minnesota recovered the bell from the *Bradley*. On August 10 they replaced the original with a replica bell engraved with the names of the thirty-three *Bradley* sailors who lost their lives. The recovered bell will be rung on November 18, 2008.

(Author's Note: Janzen and Scoles made several dives and used closed circuit re-breathers. They also donned electrically heated suits to combat hypothermia. The pair also developed a special cutting torch specifically for this project.)

Ironically, of all the videotape / photographs of the *Bradley*, not one piece of released documented evidence proves whether the ship is whole or broken in two. Oftentimes history evolves into a wind-grieved ghost, "divining things" the ears cannot hear and the eyes cannot see.

TECHNICAL DATA – CARL D. BRADLEY

Engines: Type: Turbine Generator Horsepower: 4,800 Revolutions: 100 **Built by**: General Electric Company (Schenectady, New York) **Year Built**: 1927 **Boilers**: Type: Water Tube Number: 2 Pressure: 315 **Built by**: Babcock & Wilcox (Bayonne, New Jersey) **Year Built**: 1927 **Dimensions**: Gross Tonnage: 10, 028 Net

Tonnage: 7, 706 Draft: 30.2   Length: 638' 9" Beam: 65.2 Hatches: 17   Size: 12' Centers: 24' Compartments: 3 (4 / 3,300 6 / 5,000 7 / 5,700)

Service: Years: 31 (1927-1958**) Cargo:** Limestone Cargo Capacity: 17,600 (Mid-summer Draft) First Cargo: July 28, 1927 (Buffington, IN) Last Cargo: November 17, 1958 (Gary, IN) **Service Speed**: 14 Mph (Loaded)

(POSTCARD – "CARL D. BRADLEY," THE LARGEST CONVEYOR BOAT ON THE GREAT LAKES") (*Calcite Screenings*)

Carl D. Bradley (*Calcite Screenings*)

Elmer Fleming returned to sailing and earned the rank of captain in 1962. Fleming captained the *Cedarville* as late as the fall of 1963. He retired in 1966 and moved to Roseville shortly thereafter. He died of a heart attack on February 26, 1969, at St. John's Hospital in Detroit. He was 53 years old.

Fleming's pallbearers were Arthur Josephson, Paul Stone, Vern Pauley, Edmund Jackson, Louis Carter and Henry Newhouse. Honorary pallbearers included James Cook, John Paradise, Earl LaLonde, Oscar Miller, L. T. Hawkins, and Martin Joppich.

Frank Mays, who sailed on the *Rogers City, Calcite, I. L. Clymer, Cedarville*, and *Carl D. Bradley*, never returned to sailing after the *Bradley* sinking. He worked briefly as a store accountant at the Calcite plant. Later he rose through the ranks in the lumber and cement industries to office manager and purchasing agent. He retired in 1990. Frank has traveled around the United States in a pop-up camper. He's also traveled all over the world, and even did a short stint in the Peace Corps. He sailed as a guest on the *M/V Roger Blough* and later the *St. Clair*. Mays now resides in Florida. He often is a guest speaker at various gatherings to relate his experience about the *Bradley* sinking.

In August 1999, Frank Mays visited the Great Lakes Shipwreck Museum in Paradise, Michigan. "I want to support the museum in every way," he said. "The plan for the Great Lakes Mariners' Memorial – to remember the fellows I sailed with and who were lost – is long overdue." During his visit, Mays was surprised to learn the Cheboygan County Historical Museum had a life jacket from the *Bradley*. Mays was awe-struck when he saw the life jacket. "I have nothing from the *Bradley*. The authorities took absolutely everything from me when I got to the hospital in Charlevoix, including my wristwatch," Mays recalled. "Everything I owned either went down with the ship or was taken by government officials."

B-R-A-D-L-E-Y F-L-A-S-H-B-A-C-K

Radio log of the U.S. Coast Guard station in Belle Isle on November 18-19, 1958:

~NOVEMBER 18, 1958~

Belle Isle – 6:00 p.m.: "Have Mayday off Gull Island. Tanker sinking. Weather bad, but if at all possible have Traverse base planes drop flares."

Traverse Coast Guard: "Would like approximate location of Gull Island to figure fuel for planes. Diverting Chicago-bound Albatross to Gull Island . . ."

United States Coast Guard Headquarters in Cleveland: "Cutters *Sundew* and *Hollyhock* proceed to area. Small boats from Beaver Island better try for it, but don't know how they'll fare in this weather."

Traverse to Cleveland: "Let us know position of *Sundew* to inform aircraft when to drop flares."

Cleveland to Traverse:
"Is Steamer *Sartori* still on the scene?"
Traverse: "Do you mean is *Sartori* there now?"
Cleveland: "I want to know if she is on the scene."
Traverse: "Affirmative."
Steamer *Christian Sartori*: "We are on the scene. No survivors or wreckage sighted."
Traverse: "We are holding helicopters due to heavy seas and winds unsuitable for search."

Coast Guard Cutter *Sundew*: "Having trouble with controlling radio. Want to invoke silence on channel except emergency talk."
Traverse: "Affirmative. Will do."

~ N O V E M B E R   1 9 ,   1 9 5 8 ~

Cleveland: *"Sundew* has picked up two survivors . . ."
***Sundew* – 9:15 a.m.**: "Sighted three bodies north of Gull Island. Taking aboard."
***Sundew* – 10:10 a.m.**: "Sighted five bodies in shoal water. Taking aboard. Inadvisable (to) launch lifeboats – heavy weather."
Cleveland (four hours later): *"Sundew* returned (to) Charlevoix for hospitalization of survivors."

B-R-A-D-L-E-Y   F-L-A-S-H-B-A-C-K

Right: A signed photo of the *Carl D. Bradley* **by Frank Mays.**
   Mays will never forget the rescue by the *Sundew* **on the morning of November 19, 1958. Nor is he likely to forget the countless interviews and**

photographs from major Michigan newspapers such as *The Detroit Free Press.*

(Photo courtesy of Mark Thompson)

(Author's Note: Calcite Screenings *has many photos of the* Bradley *at various Michigan ports.*

For the full U.S. Coast Guard report on the sinking of the Carl D. Bradley, *see Appendix A, page 197.)*

STEAMER CARL D. BRADLEY LOST IN LAKE MICHIGAN STORM

TWO CREWMEN SURVIVE ALL-NIGHT ORDEAL ABOARD STORM-TOSSED LIFERAFT . . .

Disaster struck the Steamer Carl D. Bradley, swiftly, unexpectedly, and with brutal finality. The second largest self-unloader of Michigan Limestone Division's Bradley Transportation Line sank in a violent Lake Michigan storm at dusk on November 18, 1958. Thirty-three members of the Bradley's crew of 35 were lost.

The tragic events from late on that fateful Tuesday afternoon until late the next day, stamp the 24-hour period as the darkest in Michigan Limestone history. No accident, no incident, no series of events of the past have left such a

mark as the death that came in the darkness of November 18. Even the day was dark. Skies were bleak and overcast as the worst lake storm of the season swept across Lake Michigan.

In spite of the storm, things were routine for the men aboard the Bradley. She was nearing home, the Port of Calcite at Rogers City, Michigan carrying water in ballast, after delivering a cargo of limestone to Gary, Indiana. Ironically, the Bradley's first cargo of stone went to the Gary area, 31 years before.

The Bradley was riding easily on the afternoon of November 18. Captain

Roland O. Bryan, a veteran of more than 28 years as a ship's master and officer, (five of them on the Bradley) kept the Bradley to the western side of Lake Michigan to take advantage of the protection offered by the Wisconsin shoreline. Winds from the southwest gave the big ship a following sea. The sturdy, 639-foot vessel had weathered many storms of equal fury in her 31 seasons on the Great Lakes.

First Mate Elmer Fleming, one of the two survivors, later told of walking on deck from the pilothouse to the stern for dinner. Usually in rough weather, members of the crew use the tunnel. When Fleming returned to the pilothouse everything was normal.

CONTINUED ON NEXT PAGE

3

B-R-A-D-L-E-Y F-L-A-S-H-B-A-C-K

A special issue of *ML (Calcite) Screenings* memorialized the *Bradley* tragedy. Here the vessel is shown nearing the Ambassador Bridge.
The "mail boat" is seen at the upper left.

AGAIN

S/S *Cedarville* (1927-1965) (*Calcite Screenings*)

The people along the sand all turn and look one way.
They turn their backs on the land; they look at the sea all day.
As long as it takes to pass, a ship keeps raising its hull;
The wetter ground-like glass reflects a standing gull.
The land may vary more, but wherever the truth may be
The water comes ashore, and the people look at the sea.
They cannot look out far: they cannot look in deep,
But when was that ever a bar to any watch they keep?
–Robert Frost (*Neither Out Far Nor in Deep*)

~~~~ ❑ ~~~~

CHAPTER 15

A Long Gray Ship

The years following the *Bradley* tragedy slowly melted away. From 1958--1965, the United States has rapidly changed. "Ike" isn't President. Americans have enthusiastically welcomed the arrival and promise of a vigorous, youthful, attractive man, John F. Kennedy. The promise dies when America's first Catholic president is blown away in a Dallas, Texas, motorcade. A fellow named Lyndon Johnson takes his place and faces a world in turmoil. America and Russia still are waging a "Cold War"; China is testing A-bombs, a resolute reminder of the Nuclear Age; astronauts and cosmonauts are flying above the Earth in a new, uncharted void.

And Southeast Asia, a faraway, seemingly insignificant place we vaguely remember reading about in 1958, is very much in the news as America begins its long, tragic involvement in Vietnam.

Rogers City has progressed ever-cautiously into the future. The years somehow have softened the blow of the *Bradley* devastation. Long, gray ships still transport thousands of tons of Calcite limestone to America's demanding steel mills, as the nation's technological advance accelerates, perhaps too quickly.

May 1965. A fresh, springtime wind blows freely. Another shipping season is well underway. At Calcite harbor the S/S *Cedarville* sits at its home berth. Built as a straight-deck, bulk carrier in 1927, the ship originally was christened the *A. F. Harvey* for the Pittsburgh Steamship Division of United States Steel Corporation. The *A. F. Harvey's* #255 steel hull, a duplicate of hull #269 (*Myron C. Taylor*) and hull #274 (*Eugene P. Thomas*), was some 588 feet in length. Construction of the carrier was completed by Great Lakes

Engineering Works in River Rouge, Michigan. Weighing in excess of 8,000 tons, the *A.F.Harvey* was powered by a 2,100-horsepower engine. In 1956 the vessel was transferred to the Bradley Transportation Line.

The *A. F. Harvey* before it became the *Cedarville.* Note the absence of an unloading boom.
(*Calcite Screenings*)

Rita Smith christens the *Cedarville.* (Left to right) Captain William Chain, Chief Engineer Arnold Specht, Michigan Limestone President Christian Beukema and Norman O. Hoeft were on hand for the proud occasion. (*Calcite Screenings*)

The ship was to be employed in the ever-increasing limestone trade. During the winter of 1956-57, the *A.F. Harvey* was converted to a conveyor-type, self-unloader by the Defoe Shipbuilding Company at Bay City, Michigan.

The structural transformation also resulted in a new namesake. It was renamed the *Cedarville*, in honor of the Michigan city near United States Steel Corporation's dolomite deposits. In 1960 the carrier was re-boilered and re-stokered. Sporting a "new image," the *Cedarville* was eager to continue a proud limestone tradition.

On the early morning of May 7, 1965, the *Cedarville* lay docked at Calcite harbor in Rogers City. The long freighter was waiting to transport another limestone cargo. First Mate Harry Piechan, a rotund sailor, supervised activities of deckhands as they secured sixteen hatches; then the crewmen prepared to wash down a limestone-strewn, non-skid deck. Piechan, who had the 4-8 a.m. watch, also made certain the unloading boom was secure. Everything was normal.

The steamer, loaded with more than 14,000 tons of open-hearth limestone, was ready to embark on a lake journey to Gary, Indiana. Earlier the thirty-five-man crew had bid fond farewells to families and friends. The *Cedarville*'s captain, Martin E. Joppich, 54, was a thirty-year sailing veteran and second-year skipper.

Shortly after 5:00 a.m. on May 7, 1965, the *Cedarville* cleared the Calcite break wall as it headed into the foggy waters of Lake Huron. The sailors were respectful of the big lake, third largest of the Great Lakes, as they knew perils could strike swiftly and suddenly.

Near-disaster had struck the Lakes the previous night when the 504-foot *J. E. Upson* rammed the Grays Reef Lighthouse, while the vessel traveled in dense fog, some thirty miles northeast of Charlevoix, Michigan. There were no injuries, but the collision resulted in a ruptured bow stem, forcing Captain Albert Olson to carefully navigate his damaged vessel to Mackinaw City for repairs.

The *J. E. Upson*, upbound for a Canadian port, was owned by the Marine Transit Company of Cleveland. The collision resulted in concrete being chipped from the lighthouse's base. Several hand rails also were crushed. Daniel A. Discianno, keeper of the lighthouse, reported there were no injuries suffered by lighthouse staff. The station's light, fog signal and radio beacon were operating at the time of the accident, attesting to the denseness of fog.

As the *Cedarville* continued its Lake Huron route, the fog was growing thicker as twenty-five mile-per-hour springtime winds created a choppy sea. Accordingly, the vessel sounded mandated fog signals with an automatic signal device. The *Cedarville*, like the *Bradley*, was a proud ship with years of faithful service. It was equipped with modern radio and radar detection gear.

Captain Martin Joppich, in conjunction with officers on watch (Chief Officer Harry Piechan – until the 8:00 a.m. watch – and Third Officer Charles Cook thereafter), was utilizing the RCA (three centimeters) radar and the radio direction finder to establish positions. The radar indicated readings relative to the vessel's heading and had five scales – 1 ½, 4, 8, 20, and 40 statute miles.

A gyro compass, which indicated no error when checked at the range at Calcite, also was being employed. The carrier was equipped with the usual Great Lakes AM-FM radiotelephones (manned by the skipper). All navigation / radio equipment was in proper working order that foggy May day.

The *S/S Cedarville* unloads cargo at Toledo, Ohio. The ship was converted to a self-unloader in 1956-57.
(*Calcite Screenings*)

~~~~ □ ~~~~
CHAPTER 16

Collision in the Fog

As the thirty-five-man crew settled into working routines, the *Cedarville* steamed through a curtain of fog, propelled by its 2,100-horsepower engine to a speed of 12.3 miles per hour. At 5:58 a.m. the long, low-lying carrier slipped by the Forty Mile Point Light Station as the ship continued its northwest course. The skipper initiated several careful course changes in accordance with the indicated track line on Lake Survey Chart Sixty (Lake Huron - Straits of Mackinac).

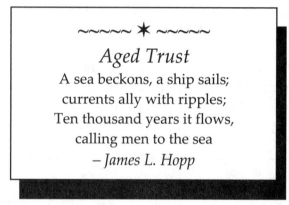

~~~~~ ✳ ~~~~~

Aged Trust

A sea beckons, a ship sails;
currents ally with ripples;
Ten thousand years it flows,
calling men to the sea
– *James L. Hopp*

Visibility had shrunk to less than a mile as heavy fog rushed to envelop the *Cedarville's* long, gray hull. Nearly two hours later the vessel cleared the Cordwood Point Buoy. Thickening gloom implored the officers in the pilot house to become more attentive to the radar. The limestone vessel continued sounding fog signals; its loud blast echoed hauntingly in sinister, foggy obscurity.

At 8:00 a.m. a crew change occurred aboard the vessel. Oncoming and off-going sailors passed each other in the doorway of the galley. Third Mate Charles Cook made his way to the pilot house to relieve Harry Piechan, as Ivan Trafelet, 56, a seasoned lookout for ships and buoys that might be lurking in the choking fog, took his familiar position on the bow. Leonard Gabrysiak, a wheelsman, professionally guided the steamer through the blinding mire as he followed course corrections on Captain Joppich's orders. Gabrysiak, a licensed mate, was at the wheel due to a surplus of officers. He had seventeen years of sailing experience.

"And a million small shrouds cloaked the day

On that fateful seventh day in May"
– *James L. Hopp*

<u>Above</u>: **Near a foggy Calcite break wall, Rogers City**
<u>Left</u>: **The** *S/S Cedarville*
(Author's Collection / *Calcite Screenings*)

In the pilot house was the engine room telegraph, which transmitted orders for changes of speed to the *Cedarville's* engine room. The telegraph had a handle which moved in a half-circle, with pointers to indicate speed at intervals of the half-circle. The choices of speed were stop, astern, slow, half-speed and full speed. Gabrysiak could also see his two compasses, the clock and tachometers. He couldn't see into the hooded radar scope in the front corner of the wheel house.

Other crewmen assumed work stations for the eight o'clock watches. First Assistant Engineer Walter Tulgetske started to blow the boiler flues to clear them of soot, a standard ten-minute procedure that must be done every few hours. Finishing the chore, Walt assigned some duties to repairman's helper, Jim Lietzow. Jim washed down an engine stanchion and painted it.

Ten minutes later he was routinely checking various stations of the huge steamer – the fans in the boiler room, the conveyor tunnel, the switchboard room, the automatic stokers, the hydraulic system. The young man found nothing amiss. Lietzow headed for the fantail where he started stowing supplies.

In a busy engine room 3rd assistant engineer Reinhold Radtke was on stand-by duty. He stood on a maneuvering platform near the engine room telegraph. The telegraph signaled all-important speed changes requested from the bridge. A large, brass bell would ring continuously until the engineer "answers." Hugh Wingo, an oiler, stood near a valve in the boiler room. He was regulating the amount of water pumped to the boilers. Meanwhile stokerman Eugene "Casey" Jones carefully watched the automatic stokers to ensure they weren't jammed up with outsized lumps of coal. An excessive coal buildup could halt the fuel flow to the boilers.

The *Cedarville* continued its lonely lake journey at nearly full speed. The clock indicated 8:42 a.m. as the ship passed the Cheboygan Traffic Lighted Bell Buoy. Visibility had shrunk considerably as the fog thickened like rich chocolate pudding. As the lake carrier passed the familiar Cheboygan traffic buoy, Captain Joppich ordered a course correction to facilitate the approach to the Mackinac Bridge Lighted Bell Buoy #1. As on previous course changes, Joppich transmitted a security call on channels 16 and 51, indicating his new course and nautical position. The ship plowed through the curtain of fog; its low-lying hull was a scant ten feet above the water line. The minutes ticked away. The *Cedarville's* rushing wake was disturbed only by dreary fog signals.

Suddenly a radio message came in. Captain Joppich communicated with the skipper of the S/S *Benson Ford*, which was sailing toward the *Cedarville*. Both captains agreed on a port-to-port passing, sounding booming signals to facilitate the maneuver. The lake giants were nearly two miles apart. Captain Joppich slightly altered course to navigate the passing procedure. The radar scope showed the *Benson Ford* approaching quickly.

Within a few minutes the ships passed each other at about one-half mile, but a thick, soup-like mire prevented visual observation. However, crewmen on the *Cedarville's* deck could see the *Benson Ford's* distant trailing wake; lookout Trafelet could hear the pounding of a diesel engine. The *Cedarville's* low, gray form continued its long, winding trail. It was nearing the Mackinac Bridge.

Captain Joppich prepared to take precautions to keep clear of expected oncoming ship traffic. A new radio message alerted Joppich. The captain of the *Steinbrenner* informed Captain Joppich that an unidentified German ship in the Straits of Mackinac was being unresponsive to radio signals. Concerned, Joppich attempted communications with the foreign ship. Nothing. Only scratching static. Joppich tried again.

Finally, after several long moments, he was able to contact *Weissenburg* captain Werner May on Channel 16 of the FM band. The *Weissenburg*, Joppich learned, was eastbound, about two miles from the Mackinac Bridge. The German captain intended to utilize the South Channel passage. A port-to-port passing was arranged.

Ship traffic was heavy in the fog-veiled Straits of Mackinac, with no less than five ships in the vicinity: the approaching *Cedarville*, the *Weissenburg*, the *Steinbrenner*, the *J.E. Upson*, anchored near Old Mackinaw Point, and another, unidentified vessel heading toward Joppich's ship. The *Cedarville* pushed against restless Lake Huron waters. It wouldn't be much longer now. The turn into Lake Michigan was only a few minutes away. Heavy atmospheric static made communications difficult; the Federal Communications Commission (FCC) was monitoring activities.

Lookout Trafelet could see only three hundred feet as the vessel churned through restless, warning gloom. A familiar noise greeted Trafelet. Fog signals. The distant noise was in the direction of the Mackinac Bridge. Trafelet reported the signals to Captain Joppich. As the *Weissenburg* passed under the Mackinac Bridge's towering span, Captain May transmitted a message to Joppich. May warned the *Cedarville* master to be on the lookout for an unidentified Norwegian ship, which was sailing ahead of the *Weissenburg* toward the *Cedarville.*

Joppich attempted radiotelephone contact with the foreign vessel. Scratching static was the only reply. Joppich tried again. Nothing. More mocking static. *What's going on here?*

"It's an eerie feeling, even if you have radar. You don't know if that radar is going to malfunction."
– Leonard Gabrysiak, *Cedarville* wheelsman

Third mate Cook warned Joppich that radar soundings indicated an unidentified target "dead ahead." Again a radio communication was sent. Still no reply. An uncomfortable feeling permeated the air. Something had to be done! Quickly, Captain Joppich ordered Leonard Gabrysiak to change course to ensure a safe passing between the vessels. The engines were reduced to half-speed. Cook, whose head was buried in the radar scope, reported some encouraging news that broke the tension. Radar bearings of the foreign ship were widening; hence a safe passing seemed assured.

But the *Cedarville's* sudden, unplanned course change presented Joppich with a new peril. Cook again consulted the maritime charts and rechecked radar headings. My God! The new course change had the *Cedarville* heading toward Majors Shoal, a reef formation three miles east of the Mackinac Bridge! Couldn't continue that route! Otherwise, the *Cedarville* would run aground! Third Mate Cook reported his findings to his captain; consequently, Joppich ordered a new course which would clear the ship-threatening reef. Unknown to Captain Joppich and the crew, the *Cedarville* had entered a trap.

Relieved the reef was no longer a problem, Cook returned to the radar screen. *Wow! That was close! It's a good thing that he – hey, wait a minute! What the hell is this?* Cook peered at the radar screen. The scope reflected disheartening news. The radar "blips" indicated a fast-closing target, but the readings were so erratic it was difficult to plot them. Cook relayed the information to Captain Joppich. Worried and puzzled, Joppich tried to make sense of the situation. Couldn't turn right! That would head the ship toward Majors Shoal, onto the reef. Concerned eyes scanned a forlorn sea, but the blinding fog offered no clues. The *Cedarville* skipper again tried radio contact. Nothing but whining static. *What the hell?*

Captain Joppich immediately commenced one-blast passing signals with the manual whistle controls. Still no sign of the "phantom ship." Lookout Trafelet reported he was hearing one set of three-blast fog signals from "ahead and to the port a bit."

Another ship was alarmingly close! This was confirmed on the *Cedarville's* radar screen, but accurate bearings were impossible. The target was so large and so near that radar readings were useless. Cook's cautious eyes remained riveted to the screen.

"It looks like he's over here pretty close," Cook remarked, as the two images moved nearer . . . nearer . . . nearer! Crewmen alertly strained their eyes to locate the mysterious, unresponsive ship. Where in the hell was it? A dismal, dreary, foggy haze stared callously back at them. Ship whistles shrieked loudly into the mist. It seemed like a game of "cat and mouse." And the *Cedarville* was the mouse. The cold wind whispered a telltale warning as the fog shrouded its secret. Seconds ticked away. A long, ear-shattering blast created war with the air. More long seconds passed. A piercing cry broke the tension.

"There she is!" Trafelet screamed suddenly. In a suspended moment, incredulous yet tinged with horror, the men in the *Cedarville's* pilot house observed a dark, hazy shadow looming in the cold mist, a ghostly specter from the deep. Leonard Gabrysiak observed a tall bow coming toward the *Cedarville*, about forty-five degrees on the port side. *Holy Jesus!* Barely one hundred feet separated the ships! The brass bell rang continuously in the *Cedarville's* engine room. **SLOW AHEAD!** Captain Joppich stared intently at the distance separating the converging vessels. It was shrinking too damned fast!

"'Hey, Dave, look at this,' said Jerome Kierzek, a *Cedarville* porter. He was pointing toward the front of the *Cedarville*. . . As I turned to look forward, the *Cedarville* blew a long signal, and I could see another ship come out of the fog, headed for our port side."
– Dave Erickson, *Cedarville* porter

"Cap, we're going to be hit!" Cook warned loudly. Joppich already knew it. He quickly ordered emergency, evasive maneuvers and placed the engines on full ahead! But it was too late! The close distance precluded avoidance of a collision. With lumps in their throats, *Cedarville* crewmen watched helplessly; an ice-strengthened, rakish bow knifed into their low-lying carrier, abreast of its seventh hatch, on the port side.
WHAM! SCCCRRREEEEUUUNCH!
A metal-tearing concussion echoed into the choking mist. Dreary fog continued to dominate the air, confirming its ignorance. The "mystery ship" was embedded only briefly in the Calcite limestone carrier, as the forward motion of the *Cedarville* swept the Norwegian ship's bow around. The captain of the vessel which had struck the *Cedarville* consulted his radar. His original heading was 108 degrees; now it was an incredible 37 degrees! Both vessels lost visual contact as they were swallowed by dense, eyeless fog.

~~~~ ❑ ~~~~

CHAPTER 17

Rush for the Beach

The general alarm shrieked loudly on the *Cedarville.*
Crewmen realized something was wrong! Captain Joppich stopped
the engines. Hurriedly, he checked various stations of the ship.
Thank God! No one was injured! His thoughts rushed quickly; he
ordered the port anchor lowered. A Mayday message was transmitted
to the Coast Guard. Chief Officer Piechan went to assess the damage.
The *Cedarville* had received a moderate jolt, and Harry wondered
whether the impact had created a major wound.

Cautiously, he peered over the port side. He was taken briefly
aback. A jagged, twenty-foot gash stared wickedly back at him.
Worse, there was damage below the water line! The *Cedarville's* #2
cargo hold was being flooded. And only the limestone cargo was
acting as a "deterrent."

The ship, a few minutes after impact, started listing to port.
As Piechan regarded the damage, Captain Joppich hailed
Weissenburg captain Werner May to learn the identity of the
Norwegian ship. Neither one knew the name of the ship which had
struck the *Cedarville.*

On board the damaged carrier, crewmen calmly performed
their duties. Chief Engineer F. Donald Lamp, who was in his cabin
when he felt the jolt, went to the engine room a few minutes after the
collision. He was assisted by Walter Tulgetske. Lacking immediate
pumping orders from the bridge, Tulgetske went topside to assess the
damage. He returned to the engine room, where he recommended the
pumps be activated; therefore, pumping was commenced immediately
on the *Cedarville's* #4 port-side and bottom tank. The main ballast

device was a sixteen-by-fourteen-inch electric pump. One minute passed. Then two. The pump noisily battled the incoming water. Another minute. Suddenly an order came in from the bridge: ballast the starboard side. Consequently, the electric pump was deactivated as the ballast manifold valves were adjusted to pump water into a starboard tank.

Everything was under control in the engine room. No panic. No expectations the *Cedarville* was in imminent danger of sinking. Tulgetske, after completing assistance with pumping operations, prepared to leave the engine room.

Upon departing, he looked at the inclinometer. *Hmm – six inches to port* (one degree). He stopped briefly at the fantail, where he further tightened some leaking "dogs" on the gangway side port.

Looming through an eerie fog, this "mystery ship", later identified as the Norwegian *M/V Topdalsfjord*, struck the *Cedarville* in the Straits of Mackinac on May 7, 1965. An 11-foot gash in her bow caused more than $30,000 in damages.

At some undetermined time following impact, Captain Joppich ordered engine room personnel to cease ballasting operations. The counter-flooding maneuver had paid dividends: the *Cedarville* had assumed an encouraging even keel. Sailors remained at their posts. No panic or desperate dashes to escape. Nothing like on the *Bradley* when that deadly, wintry November witch would accomplish its gruesome task with amazing rapidity. In fact, a carefree attitude was in evidence.

Below the *Cedarville's* massive deck, the seasoned crew – trying to cover the twenty-foot gash with an emergency crash tarpaulin – joked about how they would have to spend another couple of months making repairs. That confidence, however, was deceiving. A grim-faced Harry Piechan reported the large wound to Captain Joppich. The vessel was taking on a tremendous volume of water.

A rough graphic of the *Cedarville's* port-side damage, abreast of its seventh hatch. An attempt to put a collision mat over the hole failed.

"Cap, there's a pretty good gash in her," Piechan warned. "I tried to put the tarpaulin (a sixteen-foot collision mat) over her, but I couldn't. She's ruptured in the cargo hold."

Tons of swirling Lake Huron water filled the *Cedarville's* limestone-laden hold. Realizing his ship had suffered a major, potentially dangerous wound, Joppich acted quickly. He ordered the port anchor raised. But something was wrong; the anchor refused to budge. It was stuck on the bottom of the lake! Captain Joppich immediately reversed the engines in an effort to pull the anchor free. Finally, the anchor released its grip; the *Cedarville* was free of its temporary prison.

Captain Joppich had a plan. He would direct his stricken vessel toward the beach at Mackinaw City. They weren't that far from shore. And beaching the massive steamer seemed a logical choice. The captain radioed his intention to the Coast Guard at 10:11 a.m., nearly twenty-five minutes after the accident. Joppich consulted Third Officer Charles Cook for the proper beaching course. Cook recommended a 140-degree heading. Steering the vessel hard left, Leonard Gabrysiak steadied the *Cedarville* on the recommended course. Joppich ordered full speed ahead!

"Mayday! Mayday!" he shouted. The beaching course was set to avoid the *J.E. Upson*, which was anchored somewhere near Old Mackinaw Point. With heavy fog and choppy seas leering his every attempt, Joppich repeated his Mayday broadcast while instructing the *Weissenburg* to stay out of his way. The stricken ship plowed through the foggy mist. It seemed to be laboring. The *Cedarville* was settling considerably. Captain Joppich checked his vessel's speed. Only six miles per hour! As the giant carrier continued its push toward shallow water, two lifeboats were swung out and were being lowered to the spar deck bulwark. Deck watchman Robert Bingle was helping to lower the life saving vessels. Everyone and everything seemed in control. Bingle went to his room. He picked up his wallet and several packs of cigarettes then returned to the port-side lifeboat.

Other crewmen mustered on deck. Engine room and on-duty personnel remained busy. The men topside stood and awaited further orders. They wore orange-colored life jackets. Two, 40-man life boats stood by, ready to be lowered. Three life preservers were brought to the pilot house, but only Leonard Gabrysiak immediately secured the precious jacket. The clock inched on as the settling vessel continued its mad rush for the beach, battling the tons of water invading her ruptured hold. Yet the *Cedarville* continued to ride the choppy seas quite well. In fact, things were going smoothly. No immutable danger signs – yet.

By God! We're going to make it!

All visible evidence supported their thoughts. The long ship probed the resisting sea as the *Cedarville* rushed for hopefully approaching shoal water. Ribbons of fog wisped eerily around them.

"Get ready," Captain Joppich stated calmly. The great ship settled even more as the forward speed of the *Cedarville* lessened. Seconds ticked away. Still no sign of the beach! Maybe there would be no sign. The choking veil made them feel like they were lost in a jungle, trying to find their way through a maritime maze. Only Joppich didn't have time to consider the myriad of possibilities. The damp, cool air seemed to be closing in on the men, clouding their thoughts. More water. Ever-decreasing speed.

"It doesn't look like she's going to make it," Joppich tersely informed Cook and Gabrysiak.

His observation was cruelly prophetic. With little freeboard remaining, the carrier began tilting heavily to starboard! It was starting to roll over! The water had accomplished its goal.

Wheelsman Leonard Gabrysiak knew his navigational prowess was no longer needed. He hurriedly secured a ring buoy. Leonard raced to the port wing. The *Cedarville* was now listing horribly, nearly forty degrees to starboard!

Gabrysiak realized the ship was finished. He glanced at the pilot house. Charles Cook and Martin Joppich were trying to secure their life jackets, but the rushing water wasn't allowing them much time to complete the task. Clutching the ring buoy, Gabrysiak took one look at the water. He jumped.

"I was pinned underneath as she rolled over. I thought I would get stuck in the steel cables. I remember thinking I might get caught up in the undertow of the Straits."
–Leonard Gabrysiak

Other seamen desperately attempted to escape the sinking vessel. Seaman Robert Bingle raced across the deck and jumped into the lake. The *Cedarville's* massive deck was becoming awash as crewmen tried to launch the port and starboard lifeboats. Several sailors were successful in launching the port lifeboat. With several crewmen clambering aboard, the vessel floated free as the *Cedarville* began sinking beneath it.

Dismayed sailors were having trouble with the starboard lifeboat – it refused to release from its cables! The lifeboat stubbornly remained attached to the tilting carrier.

A once-tranquil scene evolved into scurrying madness as the great carrier listed even more. Stokerman Eugene "Casey" Jones came racing out on the deck. He tried to climb aboard the starboard lifeboat. Deck watchman Ed Brewster extended Jones a hand. Suddenly a large wave washed down the deck, engulfing Jones as he disappeared from sight. The starboard lifeboat refused to release; Ed Brewster and others were thrown into the lake. A wall of water smashed Captain Joppich back into the pilot house as he was attempting to leave it. He flailed his arms instinctively.

Second Assistant Engineer Harry Bey scrambled to the top deck just as the ship was capsizing. Swirling currents smashed into him, ruthlessly washing him into one of the vessel's rooms. Gushing water rapidly began filling the room. But there was still air toward the top! Bey looked wildly around. Harry wondered where the hell he was, but it looked like the dining room. But he wasn't sure. Desperately, he looked for a means of escape. Alertly, he noticed a port hole. Bey quickly opened it and started to crawl through.

About halfway through, Bey stopped. Jesus! His life preserver was too large for the opening! Harry was wedged in the damned hole! Hissing water filled the remaining empty rooms. *Got to . . . get . . . the hell outta here!* Some long seconds passed. But the gods were good. Harry Bey finally managed to squirm through! The call to abandon ship had never been given. Most *Cedarville* crewmen were thrown into chilling, fog-shrouded water.

"Oh hear us when we cry to thee
For those in peril on the sea . . ."
–William Whiting

On May 7, 1965, a foreign ship struck the *Cedarville* in a dense fog in the Straits of Mackinac. The collision occurred about 6, 600 feet from the south tower of the Mackinac Bridge (Lake Huron side). (Author's Collection)

~~~~~ ☐ ~~~~~

CHAPTER 18

Familiar Vigil

The U.S. Coast Guard was in full flight. Another search and rescue operation. Had it been almost seven years already? But conditions were far different.

Fog-shrouded air instead of an angry witch. Calmer Mayday dispatches instead of mandated desperate pleas. Daylight search opportunities rather than dreaded choking darkness. Two rescue craft were dispatched from Mackinac Island at 9:55 a.m. Other rescue vehicles raced toward the scene.

E. G. Dagwell, a marine radio operator, told the Coast Guard about the last communication the flooding vessel had sent: "The *Cedarville* is sinking!" The Coast Guard cutter *Mackinaw* was on its way, arriving in the Straits of Mackinac shortly after noon to assume command of search and rescue operations.

But there were considerable developments before the *Mackinaw*'s arrival. As the *Cedarville* was settling into a final resting place, the cold sea became an instant enemy to the confused sailors. Thirty-seven degree waters were chilled by forty-one degree air temperatures. Twenty-five mile-per-hour winds coaxed rolling waves. No twenty or thirty-foot monsters to cope with. No smothering darkness.

Yet the scene was eerie. Clouds of dense fog, invigorating yet deadly water, chilling, lilting winds, echoing fog horns. Distant cries for help pierced the cold air.

Cedarville Captain Martin Joppich floated precariously on the restless waters of Lake Huron. Somehow – he didn't know how – he had managed to escape the sinking limestone carrier. The skipper forlornly witnessed the death of his ship as it slowly settled into the sea. His quivering ears heard familiar voices pleading for help.

Other *Cedarville* sailors watched helplessly. It was unreal. Earlier they were on the *Cedarville*, performing work routines. Now they were in an alien environment, fighting for survival. Their sad eyes surveyed the once-proud ship. The keel and propeller stuck unnaturally out of the water. Gushing, gurgling gasps protested the coming of the end.

> **"It was so cold. I think there might have even been some ice still in the water. I got to the life raft right away. But the cold bothered my legs and knees the most."** – Chester Felax

Leonard Gabrysiak was extremely cold. His shivering body tried to fend off the shock waves which raced through him. He tried to get a bearing of his location. Damn! The sinking ship was much too close for comfort. Couldn't stay there! The suction of the sinking hulk surely would drag him to the lake bottom! Leonard tried desperately to swim from the settling carrier. But the cold numbness made it seem like everything was moving in slow motion.

A persistent, tugging attacked his legs. The swirling suction was engulfing, pulling him toward Lake Huron's floor! Rushing, frenzied water invited him to join the *Cedarville* in a final, quiet resting place. *Hail Mary, full of grace . . .* The downward plunge continued, a seemingly endless, bubbling drag. Gabrysiak pushed instinctively toward the surface. Leonard's tiring arms worked methodically as a magnet-like suction pulled at his kicking legs. *The Lord is with thee . . .* Icy water assaulted his water-clenched eyes as the whirlpool continued its madness. He couldn't take much more. Hot, pulsing lungs pleaded for air. Suddenly he shot through the water line. His shoulders were numb and weak, as the tingling aftershock raced through his body. But Leonard Gabrysiak was alive – at least he thought so. His limp body floated through clouds of doubt. Ship whistles wailed in the distance. And it was so cold . . . The blinding fog hung in haunting folds, shrouding the air with dampness and doubt. More shrieking whistles. More distant pleas for help from his fellow sailors.

Robert Bingle broke through the murky surface after his shallow plunge into cold, swirling water. He realized the *Cedarville* had been doomed. The last thing Bob had seen was the ship's propeller going around. Glancing about, he observed a raft a few yards away. Bingle swam toward it and hauled his drenched body aboard. Within minutes a commotion disturbed his rest. Second mate Stanley Rygwelski weakly crawled aboard the raft. Several crewmen soon joined them.

"I didn't really get cold right away. But after I was in the life raft, I looked down, and my hands were blue."
– Robert Bingle

The raft drifted uncertainly through the gloom. The survivors could see only fifty feet ahead. A plethora of sounds engulfed them. Baritone fog horns. Shrieking whistles. It seemed as if a thousand ships were out there. But the fog controlled the air, hiding the raft, a well-kept secret. Distant cries pierced the scene like a wailing bird. Guided by weakening pleas, the men were able to find about a dozen stunned, frightened seamen.

The German vessel *Weissenburg* cautiously floated in the foggy veil. It had been following the *Cedarville's* last reported 140-degree heading. Ever wary of the fog, Captain Werner May's squinting eyes surveyed a dirty seascape. Abruptly, his scanning eyes stopped. There, in the hazy distance, was the faint outline of a sinking ship! And then it was gone. Distant hissing filled the air. Again, May scanned the foggy wasteland. Nothing more in sight. Minutes ticked on. Suddenly, May's forward lookout reported some movement in the cluttered distance. Captain May riveted his stare in that direction. There, about fifty feet in the haze, was a floating object. The *Weissenburg* stopped. A small raft approached the Goliath-like ship. Great joy! Survivors! A Jacob's ladder was lowered along the side of the Weissenburg. German crewmen quickly pulled the *Cedarville* survivors aboard. Guided by more cries, May ordered the lifeboats launched. The vessels were lowered; German rescuers started searching the area for more survivors.

A weathered Ivan Trafelet was rescued. His limp body was plucked from the frigid lake. The search continued. A rescuer spotted a moving form in the murky distance. Carefully, the lifeboat approached the bobbing man. It was *Cedarville* Captain Martin Joppich, clinging to a life preserver he had never put on. He was hauled aboard. More time-consuming searches.

A new sound invaded the air. A whistle. Not a ship's whistle. But a decidedly human one. The rescuers strained their ears to ascertain the direction of the sound. The whistle belonged to a numb, exhausted Leonard Gabrysiak, who was found weakly clutching a ring buoy. He passed out after being taken out of the water. Rescuers had to cut the incredibly tight crotch straps from his life preserver in order to remove it. Later, guided by more whistles and pleas, the *Weissenburg* located the *Cedarville's* port lifeboat and after life raft. More survivors!

Aboard the *Weissenburg* the survivors were immediately wrapped in comforting, warm blankets and given stimulants. Fresh clothing was distributed while soaked garments were dried in the engine room. A cursory medical check revealed all was not well. Two rescued sailors were not responding to the warmth of the blankets and stimulants. Edmund Jungman, a deck watchman, was unconscious as he was pulled aboard the ship. Worried *Weissenburg* crewmen urgently tried to revive the stricken seaman. Using "arm-lift resuscitation", crewmen worked furiously to save Jungman. Another minute passed. More arm lifting. The procedure was repeated. But Jungman wasn't responding. Dismayed eyes cast downward. All the immutable signs. Edmund Jungman was dead, irrevocably gone. No medical miracle this day. A new silence cloaked the gloom.

Fellow crewman Stanley Haske, a wheelsman, died of shock and exposure an hour later. Captain May conducted a head count. Twenty-five rescued. Two dead. Eight more yet to be accounted for. The German captain radioed the Coast Guard, giving them the mixed news. The *Weissenburg* continued the search. Later a doctor boarded the ship to treat the injured. Some crewmen had suffered head injuries. Most were in shock.

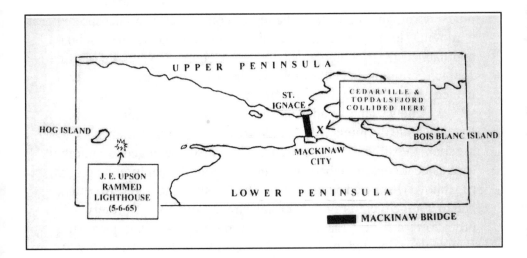

This 1965 illustration shows the *Cedarville-Topdalsfjord* collision point near the Mackinac Bridge. It also shows where the *J.E. Upson* rammed the Greys Reef Lighthouse the night before the *Cedarville* sank.

Another ship floated through the forlorn gloom of the Straits of Mackinac. It was the "mystery ship," the freighter which had struck the *Cedarville*. It had been identified as the *Topdalsfjord*, a Norwegian vessel. The ship had been sailing for Port Arthur, Ontario, for a load of grain. An eleven-foot gash revealed she had been in a fight. But damage was relatively minor. The watertight bulkhead had not been pierced; hence, flooding was harmlessly confined to the bow.

Aware the *Cedarville* had sunk, the Norwegian captain, Rasmus Haaland, worried, launched lifeboats (one motorized) to search the graveyard-like specter. Search teams located only choppy waves and thick fog banks. Around four o'clock the damaged *Topdalsfjord* sailed up the St. Mary's River to Sault Ste. Marie, where it docked at the old Union Carbide Pier to undergo inspection of damage, later estimated at more than $30,000.

Full-tilt rescue operations continued. The Michigan State Police dispatched several small rescue craft once it became apparent the *Cedarville* was down in Lake Huron. The Coast Guard cutters *Naugatuck* and *Sundew* arrived to crisscross the area. Planes and helicopters carefully flew above a dirty search scene. It seemed like the *Bradley* disaster all over again, but at least it was daylight. But the ubiquitous fog severely hampered search and rescue efforts.

At 12:48 p.m., the *Mackinaw* moored alongside the *Weissenburg* to transfer the survivors and dead. The procedure went smoothly. As the Detroit-bound *Weissenburg* disappeared into an eyeless gloom, the *Mackinaw* sailed for Mackinaw City.

News of another lake tragedy stunned the small town of Rogers City. The inimitable "No! Not again!" echoed the sentiments of those trying to forget that November 1958 nightmare. Our art class at Rogers City High School was busy completing a required project. We noticed our teacher, Mr. Robert Gertz, had a radio in class. He was being decidedly attentive to a news broadcast.

Then we were told. In shocked disbelief our class slowly filed from the room as the seemingly distant school bell signaled the end of another school day. *No. No. No . . .* Numbing shock waves enveloped our town. Two households in mourning. Eight families were now facing all-too-familiar vigils.

Mrs. Reinhold Radtke was shopping at an Alpena super market. Contemplating selections, she was approached by a family friend, Irv Saddler. He hurriedly started telling her something about two ships which had collided in the Straits of Mackinac. Suddenly an unidentified woman excitedly approached them, telling them the *Cedarville* had sunk in Lake Huron after being rammed by a foreign ship. Thunderstruck, Mrs. Radtke's legs pumped instinctively toward a telephone. She quickly called Rogers City for details of the sinking. But there were no particulars. Later, Mrs. Radtke was informed that her husband had been tentatively identified as one of the recovered dead. But the report was wrong, without merit. Radtke was listed among the eight missing. The lump grew in Mrs. Radtke's throat. Reinhold ("Reiny") had a heart condition; she feared for his safety.

Mrs. Wilbert Bredow waited patiently in her living room of a neat brick home of Rogers City. She seemed to epitomize the hopes of women waiting for some encouraging news. The proud woman related she had never worried about the hazards of lake duty. Her husband, Wilbert, a *Cedarville* steward and thirty-year sailing veteran, had not yet been located.

"Until the *Bradley* went down, there's never been an accident like this before," she stated grimly. Mrs. Bredow related how earlier that day she had taken her husband to Calcite to board the steamer. She routinely watched him go aboard the ship as wisps of fog trailed after him. "I thought nothing of it," she recalled. "The lake was calm; there was fog, but that didn't bother me. Only storms bother me. And then I heard that the ship had sunk. At five o'clock two men from the company came to tell me that my husband was missing. I'm not thinking anything. I'm waiting for the company to tell me."

Harry Edmonds (Brege) was working at radio station WHAK, Rogers City's "Voice of the North." Harried and hectic in the heat of the moment, Brege related, "We've been chasing around here like crazy. The sad part of it is, the families don't know. It seems beyond tragedy that this has happened twice here in seven years. It's an incredible average for one shipping line."

In the foggy Straits of Mackinac, search teams continued efforts to locate missing crewmen. As rescue ships floated through a ghostly veil, the *Mackinaw* approached Mackinaw City. Ambulances and reporters had assembled at the William Shepler Marina. Expectantly, they awaited the cutter's arrival. But they soon learned the *Mackinaw* would not be docking there. Hurriedly, they moved to the old State Ferry Dock, where the ship had decided to dock because of deeper water.

These *Cedarville* survivors (left to right), Jerome Kierzek, Ralph Przybyla and Stanley Mulka, are transferred from the *Weissenburg* to the *Mackinaw*.
(Photo appeared in *The Alpena News,* courtesy of the *Cheboygan Tribune)*

Onlookers curiously crowded the area as Father Linus Schrems went quietly aboard the *Mackinaw*. Many wondered what all the commotion was about. Two flag-draped stretchers showed it was not a festive occasion. Survivors were transported immediately to Cheboygan Community Memorial Hospital. The facility, a crisp, clean calm-looking building, was the site of busy activity that day. Mrs. Bethalie Thompson, hospital administrator, notified staff of the impending emergency.

But events progressed quite smoothly. Only five seamen required hospitalization (Harry Bey, 2nd asst. engineer, William Friedhoff, oiler, Leonard Gabrysiak, wheelsman, Angus Domke, watchman, Ivan Trafelet, watchman). Others were examined in the outpatients' area. Dr. Nicholas Lentini examined the men. Most had suffered superficial contusions and abrasions. A few had severe back and shoulder pains. Psychological damage, however, could not be gauged. Asked about the chances of the eight missing *Cedarville* crewmen, Dr. Lentini replied somberly, "No one could survive the cold water this long."

The second floor ward of Cheboygan Community Memorial Hospital bustled with activity. Personnel shouted orders. Orderlies paced purposefully in and out of rooms. Shocking white uniforms danced through hallways. From his warm hospital room, Ivan Trafelet talked to reporters. The *Cedarville* lookout said he was on watch duty at the time of the collision.

"It was extremely foggy. Then the other ship was about a half-a-block away. I watched it come . . . got a life jacket . . . checked to see how bad the damage was – there was damage right on deck." Then he told newsmen how he had waited in the cold water nearly half-an-hour before being rescued. "We were awfully lucky that the German ship was so near. I had swallowed a lot of water and had just about 'had it'. They had to lift me into the boat."

Following Trafelet's interview, newsmen turned to photograph Harry Bey in the next bed. He was silent but managed a smile for his wife, who was at Harry's bedside. Mrs. Bey also grinned, commenting it was "hard after crying all morning."

The hospital remained busy. Two city police cars were summoned to control the influx of cars that congested hospital parking lots. News people crowded the disaster and hospital scenes. Reporters and photographers persistently tried to secure details; even four reporters from the Huntley-Brinkley NBC news team were there.

County Coroner Harold Ireland supervised the transfer of the dead *Cedarville* crewmen. The body of Stanley Haske was taken to the N. J. Christian Funeral Home in Cheboygan before it was transferred to Rogers City. Edmund Jungman's body was driven to the Schneider Funeral Home in Indian River, Michigan. Later it was transferred to Sorenson's Funeral Home in Grayling, Michigan. Jungman, one of the few crewmen not from Rogers City, listed his hometown as Frederic, Michigan.

The search and rescue pattern continued. Eight missing. No trace of them. Cloudy doubts shrouded the restless waters of Lake

Huron. A strange, tomb-like silence was everywhere. Anxious wives awaited encouraging news. Telephones jingled consistently. Worried voices quickly answered as adrenalin rushed through quivering bodies. It was like that stormy November night all over again. Twice? Within seven years? It seemed to defy logic. Was history repeating itself?

Cedarville survivors Harry Piechan, Dave Erickson, and Billy Holley. Today Erickson is director of the Great Lakes Lore Maritime Museum in Rogers City. (Photo appeared in *The Alpena News,* courtesy of the *Cheboygan Tribune)*

Two known dead. Possibly more. One of the recovered dead, Stanley Haske, had been a seaman for more than eighteen years. It was believed he had planned quitting lake duty in June. His retirement came a month earlier than planned. Mrs. Haske's sister, Cecelia Krawczak, had lost her husband Joseph when the *Bradley* went down. Yet the community of Rogers City bravely endured. Patience was a ritual. At least the weather wasn't a merciless, brewing November witch. But the Grace of God was becoming a central thought again.

~~~~ ❏ ~~~~

CHAPTER 19

Death . . . and Life

Subdued quietness. The air seemed so heavy. Not with atmospheric pressure. But emotion. Words were difficult to come by. It all seemed like a terrible nightmare. Only we weren't sleeping. Fifty-four-year-old Rogers City Mayor Karl Vogelheim slowly puffed his pipe. A hot cup of coffee was readily within reach. A radio blared reports in the quietness. Karl's brother Ken had been mayor during the dark days of November 1958. In a subdued monotone Karl commented on the tragedy.

"The town was all wrapped up in this musical comedy (the Kiwanis Club-sponsored production of Victor Herbert's operetta 'Red Mill') that we're putting on at the high school, and this is the last night. They're not going to call it off; there wouldn't be much use. There isn't anybody who feels that the Bradley ships are jinxed; this is a thing that could have happened on the highway outside of town in a dense fog like that. You could get yourself six or eight killed that way, easy."

Betty Claus, who played Gretchen, the burgomaster's daughter in 'Red Mill', was reticent to perform in the wake of disaster.

"Father Smith – he's our director and a real professional – gave us a pep talk," said Betty. "He said that we'd have to forget what happened, forget our personal feelings until the job was done. When the first laugh came through, it was a real good feeling. If it hadn't come, I think we – the cast I mean – would have cried."

Bill Zinke worked at the Rogers City Servicemen's Club. On Saturday morning he went outside and raised the American flag in the springtime air. Bill figured the mourning wouldn't start until Monday. Later a radio broadcast informed him Mayor Vogelheim had proclaimed a 30-day mourning period. Zinke went back outside and slowly lowered the flag to half-staff.

Debby Jachick, a blond, chubby youngster, rode her bike down to the park. She busily played on the swings. Sometimes she played with the older Haske boys, but they weren't there Saturday morning. Their father was dead. They were at home that day.

One of the survivors, Jim Lietzow, had been sailing only eighteen days on the *Cedarville* when the mishap occurred. He recalled the last, fateful moments aboard the ship.

"I was in the engine room when the jolt came; it wasn't bad, but I knew right away that we had collided with someone. I ran up on deck, and the captain told us to get our life preservers on. We got the lifeboats ready to go and stood by while the captain had her on 'full ahead', trying to beach her, trying to reach the shore.

"She tilted a little, but we stood by. Then, all of a sudden, she started going over. I tried to get into a lifeboat, but I missed and fell into the water. I swam about fifty yards, I guess, to a raft. The water was pretty cool, I'll tell you. Everyone was hollering for help, but I thought we did pretty well – there was no panic."

(Author's Note: Bay City Times *news editor-photographer Dick Hardy and writer Dave Rogers flew north in a plane piloted by Dr. James C. Cooper, just after the* Cedarville-Topdalsfjord *collision in the Straits of Mackinac. The fog forced the plane to a land at Pellston, where the two* men *rented a car to drive to Mackinaw City. They then rented a fishing boat to reach the sinking site.*

Hardy and Rogers recalled crossing the Mackinac Bridge in fog so dense that they couldn't see the steel structure of the bridge. They also recalled something else: the haunting, continual blasts of the fog horn at Mackinaw City.)

More crisscross search patterns. Many voiced concern that some of the missing crewmen might have been trapped inside the *Cedarville* as it rolled over and sank. U. S. Steel Corporation hired professional divers to probe the damaged hulk, which was lying in about one hundred feet of water. Seven divers worked from a 140-foot barge. They were assisted by fourteen men. A portable decompression chamber was part of the barge's equipment. The tug *Joe Van*, owned by the Durocher-Van Antwerp Company of Cheboygan, transported the search team to the disaster site.

The diving team was split into two units – four men in full diving suits and three in scuba gear. The team included Jim Bush and Don Hockin of Cheboygan, Don Koon and Don Olson of Manistee, Don Linz and John Scott of Chicago, and Francis Felhofer of Sturgeon Bay, Wisconsin.

Fully equipped, the divers began an icy plunge toward the sunken, ghostlike broken hulk. Initial searches revealed the *Cedarville* was lying on its starboard side at a forty-five degree angle, one mile east of Mackinaw City, about six thousand feet from shore. Scuba divers searched the forward end of the vessel, while hard-hat divers probed the aft section. The task was anything but easy. Working in thirty-seven degree waters at depths eclipsing one hundred feet was very exhausting and extremely hazardous. The men staked their very lives on diving ability in uncertain waters. Progress was understandably slow. Scuba divers could stay submerged only twenty minutes; hard-hat divers were able to work an hour, but then had to spend equivalent time in the decompression chamber.

The underwater team reported disheartening news. The *Cedarville* was lying on its side in such a manner that entry into the engine room was impossible. Cutting torches were secured. Hard-hat divers took turns creating a passageway into the engine room, where it was suspected some of the missing engineering crew had been working, trying to head the limestone carrier toward shore.

The torches' bright light reflected off the divers' face plates as the wide-eyed, ever-observant searchers seared a hole through the ship's steel hull. Progress was deliberate. More waiting, caution. Minutes seemed like years. Finally an access hole was created.

Cautiously, the divers entered the *Cedarville* through the angry, jagged hole. It seemed weird. Such an eerie maze. Just a few days ago, the *Cedarville* was active, as crewmen busily worked to meet a deadline. Divers had a deadline too, but theirs was flexible. Floating debris blocked their path, but they pressed on. The divers were wary of sharp objects which threatened to pierce their life preserving equipment. Wondering eyes scanned watery rooms. More floating debris in a tomb-like quietness. Rushing bubbles engulfed sounds of silence. Then – a floating body. Then another. Yet another. My God! How many more?

The underwater search was revealing some gruesome, somewhat expected results. By noon the following Wednesday, five crewmen were recovered from the sunken ship. Wheelsman William Asam was found in the doorway of the cook's room. Deck watchman Arthur Fuhrman and Wilbert Bredow, a steward, were also located. Fuhrman was found starboard aft, while Bredow was discovered on the spar deck, under the overhang on the starboard side.

Chief engineer F. Donald Lamp was found just inside the engine room access door. Reinhold Radtke, a 3rd assistant engineer, was recovered inside the engine room, offering mute testimony of the gallantry displayed by those who had sacrificed themselves in the frantic race for the beach at Mackinaw City.

No traces were found of Hugh Wingo, oiler, Eugene Jones, stokerman, or Charles Cook, third mate. Search and rescue teams combed nearby beaches and rocky shores. Was it only seven years ago? Bois Blanc and Round Islands were sites of intensive searches by volunteers. Results were predictably negative.

Ironically, the same spring that brought death to the Straits of Mackinac also fostered life. A young lady from St. Ignace was visiting her parents on Mackinac Island. On Sunday, May 9, she felt her time was near, so the island doctor was summoned. The physician recommended she be taken immediately to medical facilities on the mainland. An urgent call was communicated to the Coast Guard. Fog shrouded Lake Huron like a funeral cloud as a Coast Guard crew piloted a thirty-six-foot lifeboat through the gloom. They insisted the doctor accompany the boat party. The six-mile trip might take longer than usual. Carefully, the crew embarked for the mainland.

Halfway through the journey, an emergency situation arose.

Not a ship in distress. Nor ghostly cries of help piercing the foggy mire. Dr. Joseph A. Soloman delivered Mrs. Duncan Graham's daughter. The infant uttered its first cries of life across the water where drowning men had given their last pleas only two days earlier.

"Life is what happens to you while you're busy making other plans. " – John Lennon

(Author's Note: One of the quietest moments in the history of Mackinaw City occurred when the Mackinaw arrived with two flag-draped stretchers bearing Cedarville crewmen who perished as a result of the sinking.

One of the first newspapers on the scene was the Cheboygan Tribune, whose offices were located only 15 miles from Mackinaw City. Within hours the scene was inundated with news' agencies.)

A Long Gray Ship (Author's Collection)

> > > C-E-D-A-R-V-I-L-L-E   F-L-A-S-H-B-A-C-K-S

In 1999, at a meeting with *Cedarville* survivors at Port Huron, Michigan, (Hans) Peter Hahn, a native of Hamburg, Germany, recalled that fateful May day. He and some *Weissenburg* crewmen were ordered by Captain Werner May to their lifeboat stations. They manned their partly lowered lifeboats while Captain May tracked the *Cedarville* on radar.

Peter Hahn remembers a "big fountain of water", about ten to fifteen feet high, right in front of the *Weissenburg*. That was where the *Cedarville* had just gone down. Then Hahn and his shipmates launched life boats to rescue survivors.

From his life boat, Hahn saw a *Cedarville* sailor waving in the cold water. But time ran out, and the man went down. Hahn remembers the day "as if it had been yesterday. The screams for help, the whole thing. It sticks with you."

THEN--AND NOW-- On May 7, 1965, the Coast Guard Cutter *Mackinaw* was a part of the search & rescue efforts for *Cedarville* crewmen. It was the *Mackinaw* that transferred *Cedarville* survivors to Mackinaw City.

The Coast Guard cutter *Mackinaw*, launched in 1944, was decommissioned on June 10, 2006. It is currently moored at the Chief Wawatam railroad dock in Mackinaw City, where it serves as a floating maritime museum.
(Author's Collection)

(Author's Note: After it was decommissioned, the Mackinaw *was within 72 hours of being scrapped in a Baltimore shipyard. A Mackinaw City citizen's group, led by Robert Schepler, saved the cutter by suggesting it be used as a floating museum in Mackinaw City.)*

<u>10 LONGEST SHIPS LOST ON THE GREAT LAKES</u>

Edmund Fitzgerald, 729', Lake Superior, November 10, 1975 **(29)**

Carl D. Bradley, 639', Lake Michigan, November 18, 1958 **(33)**

Daniel J. Morrell, 603', Lake Huron, November 29, 1966 **(28)**

Cedarville (above), 588', Lake Huron, May 7, 1965 **(10)**

William C. Moreland , 580', Lake Superior (Eagle River), October 18, 1910 **(0)**

D. R. Hanna, 552', Lake Huron, May 16, 1919 **(0)**

Chester A. Congdon, 532', Lake Superior, November 6, 1918 **(0)**

James C. Carruthers, 529', Lake Huron, November 11, 1913 **(25)**

Emperor, 525', Lake Superior, June 4, 1947 **(12)**

Henry B. Smith, 525', Lake Superior, November 9, 1913 **(24)**

(161 Lives Lost)

(Calcite Screenings)

~~~~~ □ ~~~~~
CHAPTER 20

Intensive Investigation

Rogers City, Michigan – cloaked in grief and despair.
Seven recovered dead. Three missing. Countless survivors facing the
grim specter of a psychological nightmare. Was it a dream? Another
mountain to climb, full of rocks, holes, and landslides. Mayor Karl
Vogelheim issued another memorial proclamation:

"Rogers City is again clothed in a mantle of sorrow. The
tragedy of the *Cedarville* sinking again brings to our community the
realization that we are a marine community, benefitting from the
economic returns of a worthy endeavor, but, at the same time, tied to
risk and the danger of 'men that go down to the sea.' As mayor of
Rogers City, I ask the community and the country to share our sorrow
and awful burden of loss that befalls the wives and children of our
beloved neighbors."

The community again laid her maritime sons to rest. Six of
the recovered dead called Rogers City "home." The three missing
had strong familial community ties. The sad events do not die with
the years: Father Narloch. Requiem high masses. Flag-draped
coffins. Tearful families. Shocked senses. One more time.

In the wake of disaster arose rumors that faulty radar readings
aboard the *Topdalsfjord* might have contributed to the accident. The
Coast Guard conducted a full investigation of the sinking. Lt.
Commander Arthur Gove, Captain Willis Bruso, and Commander
Thomas Powers convened a board of inquiry which faced an
intensive, complicated task. There was no speculation about a "doom
pinnacle" in Lake Huron or possible "structural weaknesses" in the
Cedarville. Preliminary hearings convened at Sault Ste. Marie and

St. Ignace. Investigators hit some snags very early in the proceedings.

There was conflicting testimony as to the relative positions and speeds of the two ships prior to collision. Somber seriousness permeated the air. It was a critical moment for the two captains. The American captain (Joppich) was in a more untenable position than his Norwegian counterpart (Haaland). If Haaland proved negligent, the penalty was a $100 fine. American officials could not touch his foreign license. If the Coast Guard faulted Joppich, he could have his master's license revoked or suspended.

Witnesses streamed to the stand. *Weissenburg* Captain Werner May testified, "I saw the shadow of the ship go under and heard the hissing as it sank. After that, all I heard were the terrifying screams of the *Cedarville* crewmen calling for help." It was then, May noted, that he ordered life saving measures which helped save most crewmen. The German captain stated many survivors had suffered head injuries, and that most were in shock. He expressed remorse for the people of Rogers City and their families.

Great interest focused on the testimony of the *Topdalsfjord's* crew. Norwegian witnesses were represented by attorney Joseph Keig, Jr. Karl Fagerli, a *Topdalsfjord* officer, testified that after clearing the Mackinac Bridge, the *Topdalsfjord* never moved more than four miles-per-hour, and more often, between three and four miles-per-hour. Yet Officer Fagerli, when asked to calculate the *Topdalsfjord's* average speed during the ten minutes it took to pass from the bridge to the point of impact two miles east, computed a disturbing figure – six-and-a-half miles per hour.

"And that," commented a U.S. Steel attorney, "is just too damned fast for the heavy fog."

Surviving *Cedarville* crewmen testified that their ship had sounded warning signals to the *Topdalsfjord* before the collision. However, the foreign vessel had been unresponsive. Chief Officer Fagerli conceded his ship never answered the *Cedarville's* one-blast signals, which seemed to indicate the limestone carrier was going to pass it on the left. Fagerli stated the *Topdalsfjord's* engines had been put on full, emergency astern, although he couldn't tell whether the ship had completely stopped prior to impact. It seemed, Fagerli testified, that the *Cedarville* was passing right in front of the *Topdalsfjord's* bow.

The inquiry inched forward. U. S. Steel Corporation initiated a lawsuit against the Norwegian ship owners. The American corporation charged that the *Topdalsfjord's* senior officers had violated Great Lakes' rules by not responding to the *Cedarville's* passing signals during critical moments before the vessels converged.

Conspicuously absent from the preliminary hearings was the Norwegian captain, Rasmus Haaland. The veteran captain had been a master since 1951. He had commanded the *Topdalsfjord* ever since it was built. Now he was suffering from exhaustion and insomnia following the horrible ordeal in the Straits of Mackinac. A physician was keeping him sedated for a nervous condition. Cynical observers drew their own conclusions about Haaland's "nervousness."

The case for Captain Martin Joppich was going well. Finally, Captain Haaland was able to testify. Ill at ease and still visibly shaken, the foreign skipper related some technical data about his ship.

The *Topdalsfjord* was built in Goteborg, Sweden, in 1959. It was 424 feet long and weighed nearly 6,000 tons. The vessel was driven by a powerful 6,200-horsepower, direct-drive diesel engine. A seven-eighths-inch-thick steel plate strengthened the bow to enable an effective breakup of ice fields. The crew numbered forty. Five were women who served in the stewards' department. The *Topdalsfjord* was on its first Great Lakes trip of the 1965 season. The vessel had sailed nineteen prior trips on the Lakes.

Captain Haaland testified his ship had departed Milwaukee at 6:30 p.m. on May 6. Its light cargo included fifteen automobiles (11 in the #3 hold ; 4 on deck) that were Europe-bound. Finished with preliminary information, the Norwegian captain stunned investigators by claiming the *Cedarville* had been traveling at excessive speed prior to the collision. He charged Captain Joppich with showing "poor seamanship" in the dense fog. Haaland explicitly stated he had seen the *Cedarville* turn in front of him at a right angle, as the limestone carrier's whistle sounded a prodigiously loud, ear-shattering blast.

"I never expected such a dramatic move to have him turn a ship ninety degrees in front of me, and especially with such poor visibility. To me, it was poor seamanship."

Haaland further claimed the *Topdalsfjord's* engines were put on full, emergency astern, while the vessel was steered hard right to avoid hitting the much-lower limestone carrier. Following his emotion-charged testimony, Captain Haaland tearfully asked a U.S. Steel attorney to convey his deepest sympathies to Captain Joppich, who also was absent from the preliminary hearings. He, too, was suffering from nervous exhaustion.

Charges and countercharges followed Haaland's bombshell. Attorney Keig demanded Captain Joppich's appearance before the board. U.S. Steel attorney Roman Keenan represented *Cedarville* crewmen. Keenan had served as Frank Mays' and Elmer Fleming's counsel in the *Bradley* hearings.

Ironically, Fleming had captained the *Cedarville* as late as the fall of 1963. Keenan invoked the Fifth Amendment for Captain Joppich. A stormy protest and controversy erupted.

"Why was he entitled to the Fifth Amendment, and I wasn't?" – Leonard Gabrysiak

Finally, a Grand Rapids federal judge ruled Captain Joppich had no legal grounds to plead the Fifth Amendment. Under federal maritime law, the American captain had to appear to answer questions.

Attorney Keenan objected to the ruling, contending that past Coast Guard policy had denied representatives of foreign flag vessels the opportunity to cross-examine American seamen before boards of inquiry. However, the court overruled the objection. Joppich underwent cross-examination.

'THE MYSTERY SHIP'
M/V TOPDALSFJORD

The Norwegian vessel *Topdalsfjord* was a powerful ship with a direct-drive diesel engine. With a steel-strengthened bow for breaking up ice fields in winter, the *Topdalsfjord* caused major damage to the *Cedarville's* hull in that fateful collision. In 1978 the *Topdalsfjord* was sold to Panama; it was renamed the *Boonkrong*.

(Author's Note: The first **Topdalsfjord** *was built in 1921 and scrapped at Hamburg in 1955. There are some photos on the Internet showing the ship which struck the Cedarville. Some photos are in color and are part of the William Forsyth collection.)*

A surprising development at the hearings was the introduction of the *Cedarville's* log, which divers had recovered from its dark, spooky interior. The log, still damp, had its pages carefully separated with waxed paper. A U.S. Steel attorney introduced it as evidence.

The inquiry dragged on. More witnesses. Time passed slowly. Still no definitive pattern as to the sequence of events. Captain Joppich testified, emphasizing the technical highlights of the *Cedarville*. He also gave preliminary evidence relative to the *Cedarville's* speeds and maneuvers prior to the accident.

Later Leonard Gabrysiak was called to the witness stand. He related his version of events preceding the collision. But something was wrong. Gabrysiak's statements did not substantiate Captain Joppich's, especially with regard to speeds and maneuvers of the *Cedarville*. Gabrysiak's testimony maintained that the *Cedarville* was traveling at full speed, almost up to the jaws of collision. The conflicting testimony further complicated the hearings. Investigators sifted through a mountain of material. The contradictory testimony of Gabrysiak and Joppich caused serious problems. Weeks passed. More testimony. Voluminous material to consider. The board of inquiry methodically and purposely considered the evidence.

The water remained restless. In June of 1966 Lake Huron revealed another rueful, unnecessary reminder of the tragedy. Acting on information that a floating body had been observed in the Straits of Mackinac, U. S. Steel Corporation again enlisted the aid of professional divers to search the area. Their survey revealed a body floating some 250 feet from the *Cedarville*. Subsequent dental examination proved the body was that of Third Mate Charles Cook. Rogers City held another funeral for one of its beloved sailors.

In August Captain Joppich again took the witness stand. The skipper told investigators he had computed the *Cedarville's* speed during the last sixty-three minutes before the collision. His calculations revealed the *Cedarville* had been traveling around twelve miles per hour – nearly full speed.

Joppich amazed himself with his own computation. "I really can't figure this out . . . I don't know why it should be that way." Joppich also informed investigators he had experienced difficulty with the *Cedarville's* communication equipment earlier in the year. Once, he said, the radar had failed completely on a prior trip.

Board of inquiry member Powers questioned Joppich about the capability of his third mate, especially with regard to competency in reading radar bearings. The American captain considered his third mate competent, although Joppich indicated the ill-fated trip was the first that he and Charles Cook had made in a master-mate capacity. Joppich stated he "had no experience with Cook in close quarters or dense fog."

The lengthy probe dragged on. Meanwhile a $15,000,000 lawsuit was started by *Cedarville* families. The suit concerned the two ships involved in the collision, plus the *Weissenburg,* which claimants contended had dispatched radio messages at critical times of call. The complex litigation continued as families faced a new struggle in the adjudication process. Months passed.

The Straits of Mackinac. A young diver swims toward the sunken limestone carrier. A ship's name plate is a collector's item. And the 18-year-old Mackinaw City youth knows this. But collectors' items are hard to come by. So is the young man's dive. He never surfaces alive, the victim of drowning.

Realizing he was running low on air, the youth had assumed that by swimming toward the top of the ship, he would be heading toward the surface. In reality, he was actually going deeper because the *Cedarville's* deck is facing toward the lake floor. The horror of it all.

(*Author's Note: In September 2003 Robert Harris, 57, of Wausau, Wisconsin, drowned while exploring the* Cedarville. *Harris was an experienced diver who separated from his diving group.*

Professional divers are quick to point out that the Cedarville *must be explored with caution. The wreck has confused many divers who penetrate the ship.*)

THE PATH OF HISTORY

NOVEMBER 18

1307 - William Tell shoots apple off son's head
1477 - First English printing press
1497 - Bartolomeu Dias discovers Africa's Cape of Good Hope
1776 - Hessians capture Fort Lee during American Revolution
1923 - Alan Shepard, Jr., first American in space, born
1928 - Walt Disney's Mickey Mouse debuts in "Steamboat Willy"
1936 - Main span of Golden Gate Bridge joined
1955 - Bell x-2 rocket plane taken up for first powered flight
1958 - *Carl D. Bradley* sinks in Lake Michigan; 33 perish
1978 - Mass suicide in People's Temple in Jonestown, Guyana
1990 - Saddam Hussein offers to free about 2,000 men held in Kuwait
1991 - Muslim Shiites release hostages Terry Waite and Thomas Sutherland

MAY 7

1657 - King Louis XIV prohibits the sale of liquor to the Indians
1660 - Iassack B. Fubine of Savoy, in the Hague, patents macaroni
1789 - First Inaugural Ball for George Washington in New York
1864 - Battle of Wilderness ends (losses: USA - 17,666; CSA - 7,500)
1888 - George Eastman patents "Kodak box camera"
1914 - U.S. Congress establishes Mother's Day
1915 - *Lusitania* sunk by German submarine (1,198 lost)
1928 - England lowers age of women voters from 30 to 21
1942 - Battle of Coral Sea ends, stopping Japanese expansion
1945 - Germany signs unconditional surrender- (Reheime, FR)
1965 - *Cedarville* sinks in Straits of Mackinac; 10 die
1970 - "Long and Winding Road" – Beatles' last American release

~~~~ ❑ ~~~~
CHAPTER 21

The Final Chapter?

Time passed. Somehow. Later a United States District Court issued a ruling in the *Cedarville* claims case. The court stated that in addition to compensatory damages, U.S. Steel Corporation would also have to pay punitive damages. Judge J. C. Connell was critical of Captain Joppich and the company. He charged that the *Cedarville* had been dangerously overloaded with limestone, and the judge castigated the American corporation for not providing watertight bulkheads in the ship.

Norwegian and American ship owners already had admitted joint liability for compensatory damages. But attorneys appealed Connell's decision, maintaining it was the first ruling ever calling for punitive damages in a maritime collision resulting in loss of life. The red tape piled up higher than Apollo 11.

Later a United States Circuit Court reversed Connell's decision. The Cincinnati court ruled that "punitive damages are not recoverable against the owner of a vessel unless it can be shown that the owner authorized or ratified the acts of the master (captain) either before or after the accident."

The Coast Guard completed its investigation and published its anxiously awaited findings. The lengthy narrative was based on more than 1,300 pages of testimony. Among the more significant findings of the 1967 report:

— **The *S/S Cedarville* and *M/V Topdalsfjord* collided on nearly perpendicular headings in the Straits of Mackinac at** approximately 0945 on 7 May 1965. The collision occurred in approximate position 078 degrees T., 6,600 feet from the south tower of the Mackinac Bridge.

As a result of damage sustained in the collision, the *Cedarville* sank in 102 feet of water, 120 degrees T., 17,000 feet from the south tower of the Mackinac Bridge, at about 10:25 on the day of the collision. The vessel is resting on her starboard rail, deck down, in two sections, and is considered to be, with her cargo, a total loss.

—The testimony of helmsman Gabrysiak and Captain Joppich differs in several vital respects as to speeds and maneuvers before collision. The version as related by Gabrysiak is considered correct, and that as related by Captain Joppich is considered self-serving and false and is accordingly rejected. *(Author's Note: As the range between the ships decreased, two versions of the events were related.)*

(A) **According to the wheelsman, L. Gabrysiak,** the course was steadied on 325 gyro, and the speed of the vessel was then reduced to half-speed ahead (50 rpms). The third mate then reported to the master that the other vessel was closing in on the *Cedarville,* and the bearing was not changing.

One-blast passing signals in accordance with the Great Lakes Rules were then sounded on the *Cedarville,* in between the fog signals, using the manual whistle controls. The last one-blast signal was a very long blast.

Shortly thereafter the *Topdalsfjord* was observed coming out of the fog at an estimated 100 feet. The engines were then placed on slow ahead (25-30 rpms). As the vessels converged, the master placed the engines on full ahead and ordered hard left.

(B) **According to the master, M. Joppich,** the *Cedarville* was proceeding at slow ahead (25-30 rpms) on course 310 gyro with the third mate keeping him informed of the other vessel's bearing and range on the radar. Within the two-mile range no precise ranges or bearings were reported; however, the tendency of the other vessel to be "widening to port" was reported. One-blast passing signals in accordance with the Great Lakes Rules were then sounded on the *Cedarville*, in between the fog signals, using the manual controls.

After several unsuccessful attempts to make radio contact with the "Norwegian vessel" and with the range decreasing, the vessel's course was changed to the right gradually as recommended by the third mate. The *Topdalsfjord* was then noted looming out of the fog at an estimated nine hundred feet. The helm was ordered immediately hard right and full ahead was rung up on the engines. When the *Cedarville's* bow passed ahead of the *Topdalsfjord's* bow, the helm was ordered hard left in an effort to swing the stern clear.

— **There is evidence that the master of the *Cedarville* failed to navigate his vessel at a moderate speed in fog and restricted visibility,** as required by Rule 15 of the Great Lakes Rules. The speed averaged under reduced visibility, from the Cheboygan Traffic Buoy to the point of collision, coincided closely with the maximum speed potential of the *Cedarville* loaded. The *Cedarville* was allowed to proceed at full speed to the time of her evasive maneuvers taken in close proximity to the *Topdalsfjord*, ignoring the considerable momentum of the heavily-laden and comparatively low-powered vessel. The *Cedarville* had adequate advanced notice of vessel traffic approaching from the Mackinac Bridge from information provided by the radar, radiotelephone communications, and later the fog signals heard. A moderate speed under the circumstances would have provided more time to study the situation and react to the collision pattern that was developing.

— **The operation of the *Cedarville* just prior to the collision,** relative to meeting and passing the *Benson Ford* at full speed after radiotelephone passing agreements, followed by the passing signals, would seem to indicate the intent of the *Cedarville* master to do likewise with the vessel traffic approaching from under the Mackinac Bridge. There is evidence that the master of the *Cedarville* was timely informed, and aware of the sound signals of a vessel not more than four points from right ahead, and accordingly failed to reduce his vessel to bare steerageway, as required by Rule 15 of the Great Lakes Rules for vessels in fog or restricted visibility.

The *S/S Cedarville* was a proud ship, with more than 38 years of service. That service ended tragically on May 7, 1965. (*Calcite Screenings*)

— **There is evidence that the master of the *Cedarville* failed to respond to the danger signal** when there was no reply from the approaching *Topdalsfjord* to his one-blast passing signals, as required by Rule 26 of the Great Lakes Rules. However as the *Topdalsfjord* (the captain) already had initiated action to stop his vessel, this failure is not considered to have materially contributed to the collision. The *Topdalsfjord* was being navigated with reasonable caution under the circumstances and commensurate with the speed and power potential of the vessel. There were adequate bridge and lookout personnel assigned on the *Topdalsfjord* for its operation in restricted visibility. At the time of the collision, the *Topdalsfjord* was practically stopped.

— **In view of radar information available to the master of the *Topdalsfjord*,** his decision to remain on course 108 degrees T., past the normal turning point for entry into the South Channel, is considered reasonable and consistent with the established principles of prudent navigation. It is further concluded that no fault can be attached to either vessel for failure to maintain a radar plot, as the various speeds employed by the *Cedarville* would have rendered a meaningful plot impossible.

— **The absence of a danger signal on the part of the *Topdalsfjord* prior to the collision is understandable** under the circumstances in the case. The master of the *Topdalsfjord* first considered the approaching vessel to be passing him safely, as determined by the changing radar bearings. When the radar later indicated otherwise, the master of the *Topdalsfjord* was precluded from blowing the danger signal, although poised to do so, by the very long one-blast signal from the *Cedarville*. At the end of the long one-blast signal, the *Cedarville* was in view, and the collision was inevitable, hence a danger signal would have been meaningless.

— **The *Cedarville* sank as a direct result of the large ingress of water** through the damaged portion of the hull. Progressive flooding of the cargo holds and tunnel space could not be controlled due to the design of the vessel and the capability of the bilge and ballast systems. In view of the *Topdalsfjord's* forward draft and the rake of her bow, it is considered that the collision did not involve the *Cedarville's* ballast piping in the number-four side and bottom tank; consequently, there was no progressive flooding through the ballast system. Since the vertical extent of the damage could not be determined, the action taken by the master to remove the port list by counter flooding is considered reasonable under the circumstances, as the ingress of water may possibly have been thereby lessened.

— **Since the master knew that, with the particular design of the vessel, any sizable hole into the cargo holds at deep draft would denote a sinking situation,** his action taken of attempting to beach his vessel is considered proper. The master, however, judged poorly the peril to his crew and vessel and the time remaining for him to beach his ship. He should have beached his vessel on the nearest shoal, or deciding against that, he should have steered the correct course for land. The beaching course furnished by the third mate was incorrect, and the master should have immediately realized this. It is tragic that the *Cedarville* steamed enough miles following her fatal wound to have made the beach at Mackinaw City.

One of the most popular dive sites in the Straits of Mackinac because of its easy accessibility, the *Cedarville* is lying in just over one hundred feet of water. A buoy marks the wreck site.

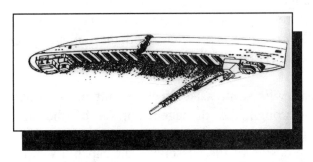

Ships avoid sailing over the wreck, as the top of its hull is only thirty-five feet from the surface. Local diver Steve Kroll called the wreck "a mess', with the ship's hatch covers off and limestone strewn over the lake floor. (David Donovan)

— **There are no readily apparent or conclusive reasons why radiotelephone communications were not established** between the *Cedarville* and *Topdalsfjord*. There are several reasons, however, that may have contributed to this: the electrical disturbances present may have adversely affected Channel 51 at critical times of call; radio contact of the *Cedarville* and *Weissenburg* may have monopolized air time; the late recognition on the part of the *Cedarville* master that a "Norwegian vessel" was ahead of the *Weissenburg*, coupled with the late awareness by the *Topdalsfjord* of the approach of the *Cedarville* as it appeared on the radar at only 1 ½-mile range, left little time for radio messages.

— **The Coast Guard units which were ordered to the scene of the collision responded** in a timely manner; however, they were greatly hampered in their operations by the dense fog which covered the area. The master and crew of the *M/V Weissenburg* conducted the rescue operations following the sinking of the *Cedarville* with dispatch and efficiency in the best traditions of the sea. It is considered that more *Cedarville* crew members would have perished in the frigid waters had not the *Weissenburg* personnel performed so well.

— **There is evidence of considerable false optimism on the *Cedarville*** that the vessel would be successful in its beaching operation. Due to this, a plan for minimizing personnel in the engine room was never initiated. The conduct of the *Cedarville* crewmen as they performed their assigned duties, notably in the engine room and in preparing the lifeboats, was commendable in that there was no confusion or panic.

The inquiry was not conducted with a "witch hunt" mentality. Investigators considered the voluminous testimony with objectivity and purposefulness. The report was approved by Coast Guard Admiral W. J. Smith who stated that "the prudent mariner must not allow habit, familiarity with route, frequency of passage, or the presence of various navigational aids to lessen his duty to comply with the rules of the road." The case of Captain Joppich was referred to the Coast Guard's Suspension and Revocation Committee. His master's license was suspended for one year, but the skipper of the ill-fated *Cedarville* would never sail again.

"When I first went aboard the *W. F. White*, it was very hard. I didn't think I could even climb the ladder."
–Robert Bingle, who returned to sailing after the sinking

(Author's Note: Survivor Chester Felax went back to sailing just two weeks after the incident. He had to force himself to overcome anxiety. Eventually he had knee replacement surgery.)

The lawsuits took several years to settle. Victor G. Hanson, a Detroit attorney representing thirteen widows and survivors, contended he had secured testimony from scuba divers that both anchors of the *Cedarville* were played out to the full length of the chains. "The fact that both anchor chains are out with long leads, that all of the chain is out on both anchors, could be a direct cause of the sinking," Hanson said. He intimated the *Cedarville* may have been dragging the anchors along the lake floor as it rushed for the beach. Hence the forward speed of the vessel would have been considerably lessened. Hanson asked the Coast Guard to reopen the case.

(Author's Note: Hanson was also involved cases related to other ship disasters: the Noronic *in 1949 – 119 dead; the* Andrea Doria *in 1956 – 52 casualties; the* Carl D. Bradley *in 1958 – 33 lost; and the* Edmund Fitzgerald *in 1975 – 29 perished.)*

Eventually the messy court proceedings were resolved. Five suits for wrongful death and thirteen for personal injury claims were settled out of court. Five men made no claims, leaving five suits for wrongful death and seven personal injury claims still pending. A final court settlement for the remaining suits was reached when twelve families were awarded $1.5 million in damages, down from an earlier $2.4 million claim.

Thirty-five seafaring men. A foggy crash. Twenty-five fortunate survivors. Eight recovered dead. Two missing. Eleven years following the sinking a body believed to been that of a *Cedarville* crewman (Hugh Wingo) was recovered.

The sunken steamer presently is lying on her starboard rail in 102 feet of water. It is in two sections, broken abreast of its seventh hatch. The forward section is lying deck down at a fifteen to twenty degree angle, while the aft section is facing deck down at a forty-five degree angle to the horizontal. It is nearly upside down. The loss of the vessel was estimated at more than $3,000,000. Its $21,000 cargo is considered unsalvageable.

(Author's Note: The Cedarville *is the fourth longest ship to go down in the Great Lakes. Divers say the* Cedarville *is in very good condition. The ship is quickly accessed because of the closeness of her keel to the surface. Visibility is usually fair, but it can turn poor, depending on the current.*

Although a lot of the ship's stores and gear have been removed [the wreck was not protected until 1995], the Cedarville *still has much to explore, including its cargo holds and easily accessible pilot house. Moreover, the forward and stern crew quarters are intact, and her engine room is now accessible. Her cabins and other areas of the ship can be reached at depths of fifty to seventy-five feet–GPS – N 45.47.13 W 84.40.13*

Professional divers caution that no penetrations of the vessel be attempted without proper training. There are many hazards aboard the ship: open doors and hatchways, entangling lines and heavy interior silt. The ship's auxiliary steering wheel was recovered and was once on display along Third Street in Rogers City, next to Mariner's Mall.)

"I think about it every time I go across the Mackinac Bridge. I'd like to go down to see it, just for my own curiosity – to see it one more time." –Robert Bingle

September 1971. Archie Goodburne was casually walking along a wave-soaked shore near Alpena, Michigan, some one hundred miles southeast of the Straits of Mackinac. His attention became riveted on a round, weathered object washed ashore by crashing waves. Scrutinizing the object, he picked it up. It was a life ring from a ship that now belonged to the ages. Had he been unaware of the sinking, he might have speculated about the fate of those aboard. He might even have wondered who truly was to blame.

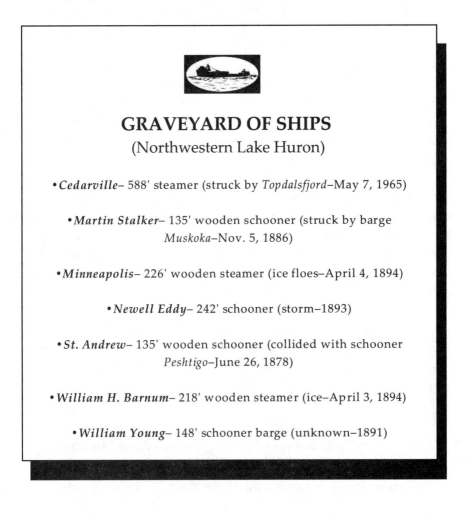

GRAVEYARD OF SHIPS
(Northwestern Lake Huron)

• *Cedarville*– 588' steamer (struck by *Topdalsfjord*–May 7, 1965)

• *Martin Stalker*– 135' wooden schooner (struck by barge *Muskoka*–Nov. 5, 1886)

• *Minneapolis*– 226' wooden steamer (ice floes–April 4, 1894)

• *Newell Eddy*– 242' schooner (storm–1893)

• *St. Andrew*– 135' wooden schooner (collided with schooner *Peshtigo*–June 26, 1878)

• *William H. Barnum*– 218' wooden steamer (ice–April 3, 1894)

• *William Young*– 148' schooner barge (unknown–1891)

~~~~~ ✳ ~~~~~

The Fear of Life

by Derrick Kierzek

A butterfly floats through the breeze of a sunlit day,
As I gently feel this reality fade away;
I'm guiding on a thought; I look to see where it's from,
Guiding through a memory and a time that will never come.
The smell hits the air like the swirling dizziness in my mind,
Like a whirlpool spin beginning to unwind,
and I'm standing at the edge, cautiously waiting as time slips by,
Clearly insane by the stars in the sky,
and I sit; and on the horizon the sunlight begins to climb,
and it seems too long since he's shined;
But I'm sure it was only yesterday – it must have been;
time has passed in front of the television.
A culture of fear cut through me, and I felt my heart contract to
my mind;
I brought the image of light, and I expanded on it;
My fear was just a shadow, and then I knew what it was all about.

TECHNICAL DATA

Engines — Type: Triple Expansion   Horsepower: 2,100   Revolutions: 83
Built At: Great Lakes Engineering Works (Detroit, Michigan)
Year Built: 1927   **Boilers** – Type: Scotch   Number: 3   Pressure: 190
Built By: Manitowoc Ship Building Company (Wisconsin)
Year Built: 1927
Dimensions – Gross Tonnage: 8,222 (Net: 6,598) Length: 588'
Beam: 60'   Hatches: 18   Size: 12 x 38   Centers: 24'   Compartments: 3
Capacity: 6/4,200   6/3,700   6/4,100   **Service** – Years: 38 (1927 - 1965)
Last Cargo: 14,411 Tons (Limestone)   Capacity: 12,000 Tons
Service Speed: 12 MPH   **Notes:** Originally Named: *A. F. Harvey*
Renamed *Cedarville* (1957) re-boilered / re-stokered (1960)
Later Dimensions: 7,973 Gross Tons (6,352 Net)

When the *A. F. Harvey* was converted to a self-unloader,
some of the above data changed.

SURVIVORS

Harry Bey, 2nd Asst. Engineer, Rogers City, Michigan; Robert Bingle, Deck Watchman, Rogers City, Michigan; Edward Brewster, Watchman, Rogers City, Michigan; Angus Domke, Watchman, Rogers City, Michigan; Elmer Ehmke, Deckhand, Posen, Michigan; David Erickson, Porter, Rogers City, Michigan; Chester Felax, 2nd Cook, Rogers City, Michigan; William Friedhoff, Oiler, Rogers City, Michigan; Leonard Gabrysiak, Wheelsman, Rogers City, Michigan; Billy Holley, Stokerman, Rogers City, Michigan; Michael Idalski, 3rd Assistant Engineer, Rogers City, Michigan; J. Elmer Jarvis, Asst. Conveyorman, Rogers City, Michigan;

Martin Joppich, Captain, Rogers City, Michigan; Jerome Kierzek, Porter, Rogers City, Michigan; James Lietzow, Repairman's Helper, Rogers City, Michigan; Arthur Martin, 2nd Cook, Rogers City, Michigan; Stanley Mulka, Deckhand, Rogers City, Michigan; Donald Piechan, Conveyorman, Rogers City, Michigan; Harry Piechan, First Mate, Rogers City, Michigan; Ralph Przybyla, Oiler, Rogers City, Michigan; Larry Richard, Deckhand, Rogers City, Michigan; Anthony Rosmys, Stokerman, Posen, Michigan; Stanley Rygwelski, Second Mate, Rogers City, Michigan; Ivan Trafelet, Watchman, Millersburg, Michigan; Walter Tulgetske, 1st Asst. Engineer, Rogers City, Michigan

(Calcite Screenings)

Presque Isle County

NORTHERN MICHIGAN'S FINEST OFFSET WEEKLY

ADVANCE

MICHIGAN WEEK

Eighty-Seventh Year—No. 19   Rogers City, Michigan — The Limestone City — Thursday, May 13, 1965   10 Cents Per Copy

Community Mourns Cedarville Disaster Victims

WILBERT W. BREDOW   CHARLES H. COOK   ARTHUR J. FUHRMAN   STANLEY HASKE   REINHOLD F. RADTKE   WILLIAM B. ASAM   FRANK DONALD LAMP   HUGH WINGO   EUGENE F. JONES   EDMUND H. JUNGMAN

Wilbert Bredow, Steward, Rogers City; Charles Cook, Third Mate, Rogers City; Arthur Fuhrman, Deck Watchman, Rogers City; Stanley Haske, Wheelsman, Rogers City; Reinhold Radtke, 3rd Asst. Engineer, Rogers City; William Asam, Wheelsman, Rogers City; F. Donald Lamp, Chief Engineer, Rogers City; Hugh Wingo*, Oiler, Rogers City; Eugene Jones**, Stokerman, Rogers City; Edward Jungman, Deck Watchman, Frederic, Michigan

* recovered 11 years later   ** never found

(Author's Collection)

The *Carl D. Bradley* (left) sits next to the *John G. Munson* at Calcite harbor in Rogers City. (*Calcite Screenings*)

Currents

Whether docked at a berth
or on the sea,
you sailed the lakes
so proudly;

Your haunting wakes did
curl and turn,
your whistles sounded loudly;
When waters cruelly claimed your souls,
we faced the day so sadly;
We prayed and wept as we remembered
the *Cedarville*, the *Bradley*;
The years roll by, the seas still flow,
as we watch the waves so cold;
Your spirits sing and your children smile,
as your story still unfolds

– *James L. Hopp*

BRADLEY - CEDARVILLE COINCIDENCES ?

* Built in the same year (1927)
* Home port – Calcite
*Were self-unloaders

* Had thirty-five-man crews
* Had the same cargo destination (Gary, Indiana)
*Elmer Fleming, Frank Mays and Leonard Gabrysiak
sailed on both ships.

*German ships were near when both ships sank.
(*Bradley* – *Christian Sartori* / *Cedarville* – *Weissenburg*)
*Coast Guard Cutter *Sundew* involved in both
search & rescue attempts
*Roman Keenan, U.S. Steel attorney, was involved in both
litigations, as was Victor G. Hanson, a Detroit attorney.

*Ken Vogelheim – mayor when *Bradley* went down;
Karl Vogelheim – mayor during *Cedarville* disaster
*Martin Joppich – honorary pallbearer at Elmer Fleming's funeral.
* Erik and Shaun Lamp lost grandfathers in both tragedies. (Raymond
Kowalski on the *Bradley* and F. Donald Lamp on the *Cedarville*)

POSTSCRIPT

The sinking of the *Bradley* and *Cedarville* is history most tragic, a glaring reminder of man versus the unpredictability of nature, as well as the fallibility of human beings.

At the core of those tragedies – "inspirational humanity." From the determination of Lt. Commander Harold Muth and other rescuers, who risked their lives to save *Bradley* sailors during a Lake Michigan night gone mad. To the courage of *Cedarville* survivors who floated in a ghostly veil, wondering whether they'd see loved ones again. To anguished, waiting families who, despite extreme emotional turmoil, showed true courage, an inspiring testament to others.

Leonard Gabrysiak is a *Cedarville* survivor. He was the wheelsman when a Norwegian ship loomed in a haunting May fog in the Straits of Mackinac as it struck the *Cedarville*, sending ten sailors to their deaths. He suffered permanent physical damage after being dragged toward Lake Huron's forbidding floor. But he has persevered.

Leonard Gabrysiak is my uncle. He married one of Paul Mulka's girls, Patricia. They have a son, Leonard, Jr. He also sails on the Great Lakes. I met with my Uncle Len and "Aunt Patsy" in January 2007, during an uncommonly sunny, snow-less day in Rogers City.

My uncle talked calmly about the two photo albums detailing the *Cedarville* tragedy. Over the years, his wife has faithfully collected many newspaper articles and photos. He frequently appears as a guest panelist, discussing his experiences of the *Cedarville* sinking, along with some of his crew mates.

Frank Mays, the only living *Bradley* survivor, is also at those public gatherings, relating his final moments aboard the *Carl D. Bradley* and the stormy aftermath. Dennis Hale is usually there, too. Hale was the only survivor of the sinking of the *Daniel J. Morrell*, a ship which split in two during a Lake Huron storm.

The *Bradley - Cedarville* tragedies remain defining moments in Rogers City's history. They recall a time when life suspended within itself, when the universe had no parallels.

But they also remind us of an undeniable reality in our lives on this planet – that tomorrow is tomorrow.

Top: Leonard and Patricia Gabrysiak at their Friedrich Street home, January 2007.
(Author's Collection)

Left: Leonard Gabrysiak, Sr., aboard the *Myron C. Taylor*, Winter 1961.
(*Calcite Screenings*)

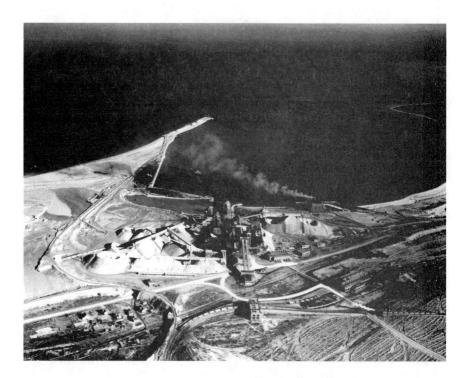

Treasures in a Museum

The Port of Calcite at Rogers City, Michigan, home of the long, gray ships. If you look closely, you can see two ships in the loading slip. In the background, Lake Huron hides the ghosts of a shimmering sea. This photo is part of the "Calcite Collection" in the Presque Isle County Historical Museum. (*Calcite Screenings*)

Treasures in a Museum

(Author's Note: The Presque Isle County Historical Museum in Rogers City, has excellent photo collections of the Bradley *and* Cedarville. *It also has copies of* Calcite Screenings, *publications which document the history of Calcite.*

Mark Thompson, the museum's curator, is one of Michigan's most knowledgeable sources of maritime history, as well as the history of Rogers City, his home town.

A sailor for over twenty years, Mark has written several books: A Sailor's Logbook, Graveyard of the Lakes, Queen of the Lakes *and* Steamboats and Sailors of the Great Lakes. (Author's Collection)

Susan (Rasche) DuBois studies a display about the *Bradley* sinking. The Presque Isle County Historical Museum has an extensive collection of local maritime history. Note the model of the *John G. Munson* in the display case on the left. (Mark Thompson)

Rogers City is proud of its nautical heritage. Whether it's a display of the Carl D. Bradley family in its local historical museum, or a memorial to *Bradley-Cedarville* crewmen at the Sailors' Memorial in Lakeside Park, the "Nautical City" is dedicated to preserving its maritime tradition. (Author's Collection)

This mural, painted on the outside wall of the Great Lakes Lore Maritime Museum in Rogers City, depicts a scene at Calcite harbor in Rogers City. Local artist Steven Witucki created the mural. From left, the tug *Rogers City, Carl D. Bradley* and the *Diamond Alkali.*

The Great Lakes Lore Maritime Museum is located on Third Street in downtown Rogers City. It is dedicated to those who have served the maritime industry. It has special displays about the maritime tragedies in Rogers City. The museum's director is David Erickson, a *Cedarville* survivor. (Author's Collection)

(Author's Note: For the full U.S. Coast Guard report on the sinking of the Cedarville, *see Appendix B, page 224.)*

They still ply the cool, blue Lake
Huron waters off Rogers City's
sandy shores, those long, gray ships,
a vestige of our nautical past, a
twinkle in a fisherman's eyes.
(Author's Collection)

EPILOGUE

As with the *Bradley*, so too, the *Cedarville*. Gone – but certainly never forgotten. Sudden human tragedy evokes a sense of utter defeat. And meaninglessness. Tragedy unobserved is even more meaningless. But tragedy forgotten or ignored suggests inhumanity.

Consider all that has transpired and ask yourself, "Had not this small community suffered devastating shock, true, classic grief, tragedy in which it was not merely an observer?"

Perhaps the ancient mariner, squinting out at the restless Lake Huron waves and sensing a sea of familiar ghosts, may have agreed. May have whispered the only thought that came to him. A simple, undying "no." And the echoing reply was yes.

ACKNOWLEDGMENTS

The author gratefully offers special thanks to Mr. Mark Thompson, Curator, Presque Isle County Historical Museum, for his expert advice, editing of text, and assistance with photos; Father Gerald Micketti, for providing a wealth of research material; Mr. Kenneth E. Friedrich, whose painting is shown on the cover, as well as in several chapters of this book; Mr. and Mrs. Leonard Gabrysiak, for interviews and providing supplemental research material;

Mr. William Ratigan, author of *Great Lakes Shipwrecks and Survivals*, for his encouragement; Randy Hopp and Jeffrey Hopp, for their valuable advice and assistance; Amy Chojnacki for her digital artistry; Mr. Richard Lamb, publisher of Presque Isle Newspapers, for the use of photos from the *Presque Isle County Advance*; Mr. William Speer, editor-publisher, for use of photos from *The Alpena News*; Brenda (Kowalski) Lamp for her interview;

Kelli, Matthew, Sheri, Todd, Franciska, David, Gracinha, Sarah, Jennifer, Amy, Stacey, Brittany and Caleb, for lighting up my life, and my family, for their love.

ABOUT THE ARTIST

Kenneth E. Friedrich, whose excellent painting of the *Carl D. Bradley* on the cover sets the tone for this book, was born in Rogers City to Herbert and Alma Friedrich. He attended local schools with Earl Tulgetske, Jr., one of his best friends.

Ken served two years in the U.S. Army. He was stationed in Germany, serving as a Military Policeman in 1951-1952.  He sailed on the *Carl D. Bradley* for about four months; Ken was a deck watchman. Then he worked at the Calcite plant, and in 1955 was employed at Presque Isle Corporation until his retirement in the early 1990s.

Ken's father was a sailor and a captain. His last command was aboard the *Rogers City*. Mr. Friedrich had two brothers, James and Clayton. James was a captain on the boats, and Clayton ran the AmVet Hall, an organization for American veterans, in Findlay, Ohio. He also has a sister, Fay, who lives in St. Clair Shores. Ken and his wife Eleanore, who reside in Presque Isle, Michigan, have been married for forty-four years. Their son Karl sails on the *Arthur M. Anderson*.

In a ceremony at Rogers City's Great Lakes Lore Maritime Museum honoring sailors lost at sea, it was Kenneth E. Friedrich who rang the bell for his friend, Earl Tulgetske, Jr., a wheelsman on the *Carl D. Bradley*.

ABOUT THE AUTHOR

James Lee Hopp, the son of Carroll and Helen Hopp, was born in Alpena, Michigan, on September 5, 1949.

A 1967 graduate of Rogers City High School, he attended Alpena Community College and Central Michigan University. Mr. Hopp taught English, history, and journalism for thirty-one years, most of them at Rogers City High School.

In 1988 he won an NBC National Teaching Award for excellence in journalism education. He was named Rogers City's "Teacher of the Year" in 1990. He has three brothers, Neil, Randy (deceased), Jeffrey, and two sisters, Christine and Carol Ann.

Mr. Hopp wrote and published *M'aidez!* in 1981, and in 2006 he edited *Virgin Forests to Modern Homes*. He resides in his home town, Rogers City, the "jewel by the sea."

(Author's Note: Matt Bellmore, Sarah Altman, Sheri Bruder, Sarah Stringer, and Derrick Kierzek were students of the author.

Their work on the Bradley - Cedarville *disasters, part of a class project, is featured in this book. Their art work and poetry are testaments to their wonderful talent.)*

Tragedy in the Straits

MAYDAY! MAYDAY!

On May 7, 1965, the S/S *Cedarville* was rammed in the Straits of Mackinac by the M/V *Topdalsfjord* in a heavy fog. The *Topdalsfjord* was a Norwegian ship, commanded by Captain Rasmus Haaland. At the time of the collision, the *Cedarville* was loaded with more than 14,000 tons of Calcite limestone, headed for Gary, Indiana.

Cedarville Captain Martin Joppich tried to beach his sinking ship but failed. Ten *Cedarville* crewmen died in the accident. Most of the victims were from Rogers City, Michigan.

Twenty-five *Cedarville* sailors were rescued on May 7, 1965. Ten crewmen perished. [pgs. (L to R) Harry Piechan, Dave Erickson and Billy Holley. Bottom: (L to R) Ivan Kiereck, Ralph Przybyla and James Malka

Top: A radar scope similar to the Cedarville's. Bottom: Two Cedarville victims are transferred from the Coast Guard Cutter Mackinac to ambulances at Mackinaw City.

S/S Carl D. Bradley
The Ship That Time Forgot

On November 18, 1958, the small town of Rogers City suffered the most tragic event in the town's history. On that fateful night, the *Carl D. Bradley*, a 639-foot limestone carrier, sank during a violent storm. Thirty-three crewmen perished. Only two survived.

Left: The Carl D. Bradley deposits its limestone cargo on shore. Frank Mays is pulled aboard the U.S. Coast Guard Cutter Sundew after spending more than 14 hours on a life raft. The citizens of Rogers City greet the arrival of the Carl D. Bradley at Calcite, July 28, 1927. Spooky view of the Carl D. Bradley's name on the pilot house 360 feet below Lake Michigan.

Carl D. Bradley Sinks in Lake Michigan

"We're going to sink! We're going down!"
—First Mate Elmer Fleming, November 18, 1958

33 Crewmen lost in sinking of Str. Carl D. Bradley

Frank Mays and Elmer Fleming, both of Rogers City, were the only two survivors in the sinking of the Carl D. Bradley. Frank Mays indicates the point at which the Bradley broke in two on November 18, 1958.

(Author's Collection)

BIBLIOGRAPHY

33 LOST; 2 SAVED
> *The Alpena News*, November 19, 1958

"Bradley bell comes 'home' to Great Lakes Lore Museum"
> *Presque Isle County Advance*, November 22, 2007

Calcite (ML) Screenings
> (May 1927, August 1927, December 1927, Spring1940, Fall 1942, Fall 1948, Fall 1952, Spring 1953, Fall 1956, Spring 1957, Summer 1957, Winter 1957, Winter 1958 - 59 {*Carl D. Bradley Memorial Issue*}, January - March 1961)

"Great Lakes Shipwrecks: Carl D. Bradley, The Sinking / The Wreck"
> *http://home.comcast.net/~greatlakesshipwrecks/*

"Carl D. Bradley"
> *http://lakefury.com/index.php*

"Cause of Wisconsin wreck diver's death still a mystery"
> *Cheboygan Daily Tribune*, September 3, 2003

"Community Mourns Cedarville Disaster Victims"
> *Presque Isle County Advance*, May 13, 1965

"Dive into the Past," 2004 Shipwreck Show
> Great Lakes Shipwreck Preservation Society

Dive Sites: Shipwrecks of the Straits of Mackinac Underwater Preserve
> *http://www.straitsscuba.com/divesites.htm*

"Dolomite and Limestone Tugs Are Workhorses At Calcite Harbor"
> *Presque Isle County Advance*, July 30, 1971

"Down to the depths in Great Lakes Ships"
> Insight, *Bay City Times*, December 12, 1982

"Ex-area man in diving expedition,"
> *Watertown Daily Times*, November 30, 2007

"First a thud"
> *The Detroit Times*, November 19, 1958

Frederick Van Ness Bradley
> *Biographical Dictionary of the United States Congress*

Friedrich, Kenneth E.
        (Interview, March 22, 2007)
Gabrysiak, Patricia
        (Interview, 1979)
Gabrysiak, Leonard and Patricia
        (Interview, January 3, 2007)
"In Memoriam"
        Presque Isle County Advance, November 27, 1958
Lamp, Brenda (Kowalski)
        (Interview, March 27, 2007)
Marine Board of Investigation – foundering of the *Carl D. Bradley,*
        Lake Michigan, 18 November 1958 with loss of life
Marine Board of Investigation – collision of the *SS Cedarville* and
        Norwegian *MV Topdalsfjord* on 7 May 1965 in the Straits of
        Mackinac with loss of life
McCosh, Dan, "Secrets of the Lakes", *Popular Science,* June, 1996,
        Volume 248, Number 6
"Our Worst Tragedy"
        The Alpena News, November 20, 1958
*Proceedings of the Merchant Marine Council (Cedarville - Topdalsfjord
        Collision)* United States Coast Guard, May 1967
Ratigan, William, *Great Lakes Shipwrecks and Survivals*
        Grand Rapids: Eerdmanns Publishing Company, 1977
Ships (Newsletter)
        December 1958
"Three Major Tragedies Leave Unforgettable Mark On Lives
        Of Rogers Cityans"
        Presque Isle County Advance, July 30, 1971
Toussaint, Warren J., "MAYDAY - MAYDAY: WORDS NO ONE EVER
        WANTS TO HEAR"
        Shipmates, April-May 1997, Ninth Coast Guard District
United States Coast Guard Ninth District Public Affairs
        Sundew Retirement Announcement (May 4, 2004)

GLOSSARY

Abreast – By the side of; side by side

Admiral – A fleet commander (or subdivision of a fleet)

Aft – Toward the back of a ship; the stern; rear

The aft end of the *Carl D. Bradley*

Aground – A vessel touching bottom in shallow water

Amidships (Midships) – Toward the center or middle of a ship

Archipelago – A group of islands

Astern – In the back of a ship; the "after end"

Auxiliary Steering Wheel – A "back-up" method of propelling a ship, usually located in the stern; used if the steering wheel in the pilot house is inoperative

Ballast – Weight at a ship's lower level; provides stability

Beam – The width of a ship

Bearing – The direction of a ship; it is expressed as a true bearing (on a chart), or as a bearing relative to a ship's heading

Bell buoy – A bell-mounted navigational object

Berth – A place where a ship can tie up, anchor or "dock"

Bilge – The lowest part of a ship's interior, where water collects

Boatswain (Bosun) – A warrant or petty officer; a "foreman"

Bow – The front of a ship

Bow stem – The forward-most part of the bow

Bow thruster – A device built into the bow of a ship to improve maneuverability (also called a tunnel thruster)

Bridge – The area where a ship is navigated

Bulkhead – Any vertical structure which separates compartments or spaces of a ship

Bulwark – The side of the ship above the deck

Buoy – A floating device employed as an aid to mark the navigable limits of reefs, channels, sunken hazards, etc.

Cabin – A compartment for a passenger or a crewman

Chadburn – Originally the name of a company that manufactured engine order telegraphs for ships; now applied generically to any such device, regardless of the manufacturer

Cofferdam – A water-tight, temporary structure enclosing part of a body of water to enable it to be pumped with dry air for construction purposes

Collision mat – A large square of heavy canvas; it has lines that allow it to be drawn next to or under the hull of a damaged ship.

Commander – A naval rank below captain

Companionway – Stairs from the upper deck to the lower deck of a ship

Course – The compass direction in which a ship is traveling

Davit – A device that projects over the side of the ship to raise or lower life boats from or to the water

Dead ahead – A position directly in front of a vessel

Deck – A permanent covering over a compartment, hull, etc.

Dock – The area where a ship rests when attached to a pier or wharf; often used to denote a pier or wharf

Dog(s) – Holding or clamping devices used on doors, hatch covers and other hinged parts of a ship

Draft – The depth of a ship below the water line; the depth of water a ship draws

Dry dock – A dock where a ship can be worked on out of the water

Fantail – The overhanging part of a vessel's stern; area of the upper deck nearest the stern

The fantail of the *Carl D. Bradley*

Fine(s) – Smaller-sized grades of a sediment (e.g., limestone)

Fog horn – A sound device for issuing fog signals

Fog signals – A series of sound signals required by COLREGS* (*Convention on International Regulations for Preventing Collisions at Sea)

Following seas – Waves approaching from the back of a ship

Forepeak – The most forward storage area of a vessel

Forward – Toward the bow of the ship

Freeboard – The distance between the water line and main deck; measured at the lowest point where water can enter a ship

GPS (Global Positioning System) – A navigation system using satellite signals to fix a position with great accuracy

Galley – The kitchen area of a ship

Gangway – A narrow, portable platform used as a passage by persons entering or leaving a vessel

Gyrocompass – A compass which finds True North; it uses an electrically powered, fast-spinning wheel and friction forces in order to exploit the rotation of the Earth.

Hatch – An opening in a ship's deck

Heading – The direction in which a ship's bow points

Helm – The ship's steering wheel

Helmsman (Wheelsman) – One who steers the ship

Hold – A compartment below deck used for carrying cargo

Hopper – A funnel-shaped container where materials are stored for unloading

Hull – The main body or frame of a ship

Hypothermia – A life-threatening condition where there is loss of body heat, causing body functions to slow down

Inclinometer – An instrument that measures the angle of inclination of a ship to the horizontal

Keel – The centerline of a boat running forward and rearward; the "backbone" of a ship

Knot – A unit of speed equal to one nautical mile per hour

Latitude – Distance north or south of the equator, measured and expressed in degrees

Leeward (Alee; Lee) – The calm side; sheltered from the wind; opposite of windward

Life boat drill – A procedure of lowering and launching life boats

List – The leaning of a ship to one side because of excess weight on that side

Log – Records of a ship's courses and operations

Longitude – The distance in degrees east or west of the meridian at Greenwich, England

M/V – Motor Vessel

Manila falls – Ropes used to lower life boats; made from banana plants in the Phillippines; will not rot when exposed to sea water

Mariner – A person employed on a seagoing vessel

Master (Skipper)– The captain of a ship

Mayday – An international distress call; "help me" (from Fr. *M'aidez*)

Mess hall (room) – A dining room on a ship

Mooring – A method of securing a ship to a mooring buoy, pier or another ship

Nautical – Having to do with boats, ships or sailing

Nautical Mile – One minute of latitude; approximately 6,070 feet; the 60th part of an equatorial degree – longer than a statute mile (5,280 feet)

Navigation – The art and science of safely navigating a ship from one point to another

Painter – A line attached to the bow of a lifeboat

Petty Officer – A noncommissioned naval officer (intermediate in rank between enlisted personnel and commissioned officers)

Pilot house (Wheel house) – A compartment on or near the bridge; contains a steering wheel, compass, charts, navigating equipment, means of communication, etc.

The pilot house of the *S/S Cedarville*

Pilot's ladder (Jacob's ladder) – A rope ladder, lowered from the deck, when pilots or passengers come aboard

The pilot's ladder hung over the bow of the *M/V Topdalsfjord*

Point(s) – A division of the circumference of the magnetic compass card into 32 points, each 11 degrees, 15 minutes

Port – The left side of a ship when looking forward; a harbor

Propeller – A rotating device, with two or more blades, that acts as a screw in propelling a boat; sometimes called a screw or wheel

Quarters – Living space for the crew or passengers

Radar (Radio **D**etection **and R**anging**)** – An electronic detection instrument; uses radio waves to find the distance and bearing of other objects

**Radar scope on a Great Lakes'
limestone carrier (Circa 1960)**

Rake – The degree of overhang of a ship's bow and stern

Reef – A group of rocks/coral usually at depths shallow enough
to be a navigational hazard

Rudder – A vertical plate for steering a ship

Running lights – Lights required to be shown on ships underway
between sundown and sunset (a red light = the port side; a
green light = the starboard side; white lights on the
foremast, after mast, and the stern)

Ring buoy – A life-saving, ring-shaped device

Rivets – Metal pins by which a ship's plating (and other parts) of
iron and steel are joined

Roll – The alternating motion of a ship

S/S – Steamship

Sea Anchor (Life Raft) – A cone-shaped, gray canvas anchor,
measuring about three feet long

Seaworthy – A ship able to meet the usual sea conditions

Sonar (Sound **N**avigation **a**nd **R**anging) – A device which locates
a submerged object by emitting high-frequency sound
waves and registering the vibrations reflected from the
object

Spar – A ship's mast

Squall – A sudden, violent wind, often accompanied by rain or
   snow

Stanchion – An upright bar or post used for support of a deck

Starboard – The right side of a ship when facing the bow

Steerageway – The minimum rate of motion required for a ship to
   be maneuvered by the helm

Stern – The back (rear) of a ship

Stokes litter (basket) – A rigid, body-sized platform in which a
   stretcher or litter can be secured for transporting patients,
   usually in precarious environments

Tugboat (Tug) – A small, powerful steamer used for towing /
   guiding larger ships

**The tugboat *Rogers City*
guided ships like the *Carl
D. Bradley* into the loading
slips at Calcite Harbor in
Rogers City.**

Transverse – Placed at right
angles to the keel

Wake – Moving waves,
track or path that a ship leaves behind it

APPENDIX A

UNITED STATES COAST GUARD

(Marine Board of Investigation; foundering of the *Carl D. Bradley*,
    Lake Michigan, 18 November 1958 with loss of life)

After full and mature deliberation, the board finds as follows:

FINDINGS OF FACT

1. The particulars on the S/S *Carl D. Bradley*:

Name: *Carl D. Bradley*
Owner: Michigan Limestone Division, U.S. Steel Corporation
Official No: 226776
Tonnage: 10,028 Gross; 7706 Net
Home Port: New York
Type Vessel: Self-unloading bulk carrier
Dimensions: 623' x 65' x 33'
Propulsion: Steam, single screw, turbo-electrical, two Foster-
    Wheeler boilers 450#
Classification: Lloyd's Register of Shipping, 100A1 and LMC
Builder: American Shipbuilding Company, Lorain, Ohio, yard,
    1927, hull number 797
Master: Roland Bryan, Loudonville, New York
Chief Engineer: Raymond Buehler, 1500 Cordova Avenue,
    Lakewood, Ohio

2. The *Carl D. Bradley* was given her last annual inspection at Calcite, Michigan, by Commander Mark L. Hocking and Lieutenant Frank M. Sperry, inspectors from the OCMI Office, St. Ignace, Michigan. This inspection started on 30 January 1958 and was completed on 17 April 1958, and a certificate of inspection was issued on that date.

3. The *Carl D. Bradley* had an established load line. The current certificate issued by Lloyd's Register of Shipping was last endorsed on 26 February 1958 by Mr. J.D.Wallace and R.S Haugenson, surveyors.

4. During the 1957-58 winter lay-up, miscellaneous cargo hold repairs were effected. These included replacement of deteriorated or loose rivets by carriage bolts in the hopper side slope plates. Although the Coast Guard had not given prior approval to these repairs, they were considered adequate by Lieutenant Sperry when he viewed the work in progress. These repairs were later reported by the Master to be holding satisfactorily, and there was no report of leaking in the side tanks during the 1958 season.

5. The *Carl D. Bradley* was scheduled for extensive cargo hold renewal and replacement during the 1958-59 winter lay-up. This work was to be performed at Manitowoc Shipbuilding Company, Manitowoc, Wisconsin, and was to consist primarily of the reconstruction of the tank top, renewal of the cargo hold side slopes and screen bulkheads, and the installation of a centerline bulkhead between frames 32 and 170, as shown on H.C. Downer and Associates Drawings YD 411-S9-3-1 (Appendix "Y") and YD 411-S11-11-1 (Appendix "Z"), approved by the Coast Guard on 25 February 1958 and by Lloyd's on 11 October 1957.

A comparison of the midship section, as originally built (Exhibit 6), and that shown on H.C. Downer Drawing YD-411-S11-11-1 (Appendix "Z") indicates that the above work would have increased the longitudinal strength by a moderate amount. It was also the owner's intent to dry-dock the vessel in Chicago after the completion of the work in Manitowoc for its five-year survey, the last five-year survey docking having been accomplished in Lorain, Ohio, in 1953.

6. The *Carl D. Bradley* was in dry-dock for period 9-15 May 1957 at Chicago, Illinois, to effect repairs incident to damages sustained on 3 April 1956 in a collision with the *M/V White Rose* at South East Bend, St. Clair River. These repairs consisted of inserting one (1) new bilge plate 21 feet long to replace damaged sections of Plates E-14 and E-15 starboard, and minor fairing and riveting to shell plates K-8 and K-9 port side.

In addition, hairline fractures in the transverse direction, located for the most part at the after edge of the riveted lap butts, were found in bottom plates B-16, D-16, D-18, D-19 starboard, and B-14, B-15, C-9, C-16, and D-12 port. These plates were repaired by cropping out the fractured sections of the plates and the adjacent riveted lap butts and inserting a new full-width section approximately six feet in length.

In effecting these repairs, the butts were flush welded and the seams were riveted. Satisfactory, temporary repairs were also made to shell plate J-20 aft on the port side in way of the engine room forward bulkhead, and the internals in way of this plate and miscellaneous repairs were also made on the starboard side aft, exact location unknown.

7. On two known occasions between the dry-docking in May 1957 and the casualty, the *Carl D. Bradley* sustained bottom damage. In the spring of 1958, the vessel rubbed bottom while proceeding out of Cedarville, Michigan, and damage was incurred just aft of the collision bulkhead in way of No. 1 water bottom, port.

The owners considered this damage to be of such a minor extent that no repairs were necessary. In early November 1958, the vessel again rubbed bottom while turning at Cedarville, and damage was sustained in way of No. 7 water bottom, port, in the A and B strakes. This damage, a transverse fracture approximately 14" long, was repaired afloat at Calcite, Michigan, by the owner's repair force by welding a channel bar over the fracture and blanking each end to form a cofferdam. The size of this channel is not known.

8. Neither of the above-mentioned damages was reported to the Coast Guard or Lloyd's, and the repair in No. 7 water bottom was neither reported to nor approved by the Coast Guard.

9. On 30 October 1958, a safety inspection was conducted on board the *Carl D. Bradley* by Lieutenant Sperry. This inspection consisted of a fire drill and a boat drill, during which both boats were swung out and No. 2 boat was lowered into the water, and 28 crewmen exercised under oars to the satisfaction of the inspector. It was during this visit to the vessel that the Master reported that the repairs to the side tanks were holding up satisfactorily.

10. The *Carl D. Bradley* was of typical arrangement for self-unloading type vessels with a forepeak and large cargo area, and having propulsion machinery aft. These areas were separated by two transverse watertight bulkheads, the collision bulkhead at frame 12 and the engine room forward bulkhead at frame 173.

The cargo hold space was divided into five compartments by screen bulkheads above the tunnel, and the unloading machinery was located in the conveyor room just forward of the cargo spaces. The entire 475-foot length of the cargo spaces was open longitudinally through the tunnel and conveyor room.

11. The *Carl D. Bradley* was engaged in the limestone and coal trade, operating primarily between the limestone ports on Lake Huron and unloading ports on Lakes Michigan and Erie. The 1958 season began on 22 April and the *Carl D. Bradley* had completed 43 round trips before the casualty. The vessel was not in operation for a period of about three months commencing about 1 July and ending about 1

October by reason of a business lag. During this period, the vessel lay at Calcite, Michigan, with only a watchman on board.

12. Captain Bryan had been sailing as Master of the *Carl D. Bradley* since 1954. Chief Engineer Buehler had served on the *Carl D. Bradley* for almost the entire life of the vessel and as Chief Engineer since 1952.

13. The manager of the Bradley Transportation Fleet is Mr. Norman Hoeft, and he has held his present position for approximately two years. He has had no sailing experience, but has been in the employment of Michigan Limestone Division for some 33 years in various capacities. His last previous assignment was in the traffic department.

14. Present management knew of no company instructions issued concerning the sequence of loading, unloading, or ballasting of their vessels. They consider that the responsibility in these matters is vested in the ships' masters. There were certain practices followed on the *Carl D. Bradley* which developed into recommended procedures as a result of the experience of vessel personnel, and which were passed on by masters and mates to their successors.

15. The Master and Chief Engineer of the *Carl D. Bradley* were charged with the responsibility of keeping the management advised as to the repairs, maintenance and upkeep requirements. The management structure of the Bradley Fleet, which consisted of nine vessels, did not provide for a fleet captain or a fleet engineer.

16. The safety director of the Bradley Transportation Fleet had not, in his four (4) years in his present capacity, received any complaints of unsafe or hazardous operating conditions on the *Carl D. Bradley*. It is noted that the safety program, as administered by the safety director for the Bradley Fleet, was almost solely devoted to industrial-type safety conditions and did not encompass vessel material

conditions.

For success in this field, the National Safety Council presented an award of honor to the Bradley Transportation Line, Michigan Limestone Division, Rogers City, Michigan, for the world's record in having 2,228,755 injury-free man hours, 24 April 1955 to 31 December 1957. The present safety director had not at any time personally made a material condition inspection of the *Carl D. Bradley*.

17. The *Carl D. Bradley* departed Gary, Indiana, bound for Calcite, Michigan, at approximately 2200 on 17 November 1958. Prior to departure, the Master and Mate had knowledge of the weather forecast, which at 2000 warned of whole gale winds (50-65 MPH) from the south, shifting to southwest. At the time of departure, the wind was fresh (25-35 MPH) from the south, and there was no sea.

18. When the *Carl D. Bradley* was secured for sea, special attention was given to the hatch clamps and boom stays, because of the impending weather. The vessel was in a light condition with the forward tanks only partially ballasted. The ballasting of the after tanks (5,6 and 7, and Trim) was handled by the engineering force, and the amount of water in the after tanks during the voyage could not be determined. However, normal practice was to have the vessel ballasted full aft to get the propeller down, and the vessel would, therefore, have had a draft between 17'6" and 18' aft. The forward draft was not measured at the time of departure. The above was the normal ballasting procedure for departing port without cargo.

19. At 0400 on 18 November 1958, the *Carl D. Bradley* passed Milwaukee at a distance of 11 miles, making approximately 15 MPH, and was abeam Sheboygan at 0700, a distance of seven miles. Two lake freighters, the *S/S Governor Miller* and *Richard Trimble*, were running parallel with the *Carl D. Bradley* and closer to shore. The wind increased steadily after 0400, and during the 4-8 watch, the water ballast was increased to the maximum practical condition of 10,

16, 18 and 18 feet in the tanks #1, 2, 3 and 4 respectively. The vessel remained ballasted in this manner until the casualty.

20.   The *Carl D. Bradley* continued up the Wisconsin shore at distances off varying from five to twelve miles. From a point off Cana Island, the course of 046 degrees true was set across Northern Lake Michigan toward a point midway between Seul Choix Point and Lansing Shoal. Sometime prior to 1600 speed had been reduced by about 10 RPM so that the vessel was making approximately 14-15 MPH. At 1519 a fix was plotted by the Second Mate from visual bearings, and this position indicated the vessel to be slightly to the south of the line drawn on the chart for the route across Lake Michigan.

21.   At 1600, when First Mate Elmer Fleming came on watch, the Master was on the bridge and in charge of the navigation. The *Carl D. Bradley* was past Poverty Island on course 046 degrees true, and was riding comfortably with a heavy following sea slightly on the starboard quarter. The wind had increased to whole gale force (60-65 MPH) and had shifted to southwest.

22.   The *S/S Johnstown*, ahead of the *Carl D. Bradley* by several hours, passed Boulder Reef at about 1317, and had reported encountering a very heavy sea there at that time. The only other lake freighter which reported passing Boulder Reef was the *S/S Charles L. Hutchinson*, which passed the reef at 0554 on the 18th, downbound and loaded. This vessel reduced speed at 0700 because of heavy seas.

All other lake vessels that reported having been in the northern Lake Michigan area at this time reported that they had sought shelter, and at least eight vessels were anchored or proceeding to anchor at the time of the casualty, either in Green Bay, at Garden Island, or in the Straits of Mackinac.

23. Sometime after 1600, the radar was placed in operation and was used for all subsequent navigation, except for the RDF bearing of 051

degrees true obtained on Lansing Shoal sometime before 1700. After the fix obtained at 1519 was plotted on the chart, no later positions were plotted. However, radar observations indicated that on the course being steered (046 degrees true), the vessel would clear Boulder Reef and Gull Island by at least five miles. At about 1720, radar ranges were taken on the north end of South Fox Island and on Point aux Barques, which again showed the vessel to be slightly right of the course line drawn on the chart.

24. Within one-half hour before the casualty, both survivors, Fleming and Mays, had occasion to traverse the length of the vessel from the forward house to the after house on the weather deck, and neither one saw nor heard anything out of the ordinary which would have caused them to be concerned with the safety of the vessel. In addition, Mays also went aft to the engine room and returned to the fore part of the vessel, through the tunnel, and, again, neither saw nor heard anything unusual.

Up to the time of the casualty, the vessel was riding easily, taking no water over the deck, and with so smooth a motion that the sideboards were not necessary on the mess table. Accordingly, persons on board were not aware of any reason to be concerned for the safety of the vessel.

25. The bulkhead at the forward end of the engine and boiler spaces, "Blk #173" was fitted with a dogged watertight door which opened forward into the tunnel. The door was normally kept closed, although rarely, if ever, completely dogged. Just prior to the casualty, when Mays was aft to pump the water from the sump to the after end of the vessel, he used this door, and when last leaving it, tightened at least one dog. The sumping of the water in the tunnel was a singularly assigned duty of the deck watch to be performed each watch, and on this occasion Mays found no more than the normal amount of water in the tunnel.

26. At approximately 1730, without warning, a sound described as

a thud was heard on the bridge of the *Carl D. Bradley*. The thud, which Fleming could not more adequately describe, was followed by a vibration, similar to that which is felt in a vessel pounding into a sea, with the propeller out of the water, but the thud was such as to cause Fleming to instinctively realize that the vessel was in serious trouble. Looking aft, Fleming noted that the stern of the *Carl D. Bradley* was sagging.

27. After sumping the pump aft, Mays proceeded through the tunnel on the tank top to the conveyor room forward, and was there when he also heard the thud, which he was totally unable to describe. However, he, too, realized that the vessel was in serious trouble and ran immediately for the ladder leading topside. As he departed this compartment, he neither heard nor saw that section of the vessel being flooded.

28. Back on the bridge, the Master immediately sounded the general alarm and began to blow the whistle, while Fleming broadcast "MAY DAY" on channel 51 (2182 kc). This broadcast, which was immediately answered by radio station WAD, Port Washington, Wisconsin, gave the *Carl D. Bradley*'s position as 12 miles southwest of Gull Island. Upon request by WAD, the *Carl D. Bradley* verified this position. There had been just enough time to put out two "MAY DAY" messages before the power failed, and the lights forward went out. There were no further signals heard from the *Carl D. Bradley*.

   The "MAY DAY" was heard and recorded by a large number of stations, including the Coast Guard Lifeboat Station at Charlevoix, Michigan, and primary radio station NMD at Chesterfield, Ohio.

29. At 1730, the *Carl D. Bradley* was still on course 046 degrees true, was riding easily and making about 14.5 MPH. The vessel was ballasted to the maximum practical extent with estimated drafts of 13'9" forward and 17'6" aft. The wind was southwest 55-65 MPH, and the sea was heavy, steep, and about 25 feet high from ½ point on the starboard quarter. The approximate air and water temperatures

-205-

were 40 degrees F and 50 degrees F, respectively. The sun had set at 1710, and there was (sic) still 14 minutes of twilight which would end at 1744.

30. The German *M/V Cristian* (sic) *Sartori*, a 254' general cargo vessel, was at about 1730 about four miles distant from the *Carl D. Bradley*, and although the *Cristian Sartori* did not hear the "MAY DAY", officers on the bridge witnessed the casualty. The *Cristian Sartori*, southbound, passed Lansing Shoal at 1200. The *Johnstown* later reported sighting her at about 1400, one to two miles off her port side, when the *Johnstown* was abeam Gull Island Light, distance three to four miles, on course 050 degrees true. This put the *Cristian Sartori* approximately five miles off Gull Island.

At about 1700, the *Cristian Sartori* came right to course 215 degrees true, making about 2 MPH, when she sighted the *Carl D. Bradley* ahead, 10-15 degrees on her starboard bow. At 1720, the *Cristian Sartori* came right to course 240 degrees true to pass the *Carl D. Bradley* on her port side, and by 1730 the *Cristian Sartori* was approximately six miles distant from Gull Island, bearing 260 degrees true from Gull Island Light, with the *Carl D. Bradley* 10-15 degrees on her port bow. The only side light of the *Carl D. Bradley* seen at any time by the *Cristian Sartori* was her red light, and at no time was the green side light visible to the *Cristian Sartori*.

31. When the alarm sounded, the crew responded quickly and sought to abandon ship. With the exception of the Second Mate, who tried to go aft toward the boat deck (body not recovered), those forward donned life jackets and went to the 15-person emergency life raft aft of the pilot house. Men aft were observed to be on the boat deck and lowering the starboard lifeboat. The two lifeboats were 25-person boats on the boat deck aft and were equipped with quadrantal-type mechanical davits, Manila falls, and common hooks.

32. Two or three minutes after the thud and after the stern had been noted to sag, the vessel heaved upward near hatch #10 and broke in

two, resulting in two sections approximately 300' in length, 65' wide and 90' high, including the deck houses and superstructure. As the sections parted, the forward end of the stern section, with the lights still on, swung to port, and the after end of the bow section swung to starboard. The bow section, maintaining an even keel, settled from the after end until the spar (weather) deck was completely submerged, then listed to port, rolled over, and sank. The life raft floated free.

33. The stern section settled from the forward end on an even keel, with the counter going down last. The starboard lifeboat swung forward on its falls. Whether the boat was completely launched before the sinking cannot be determined. When recovered, it was upside down, and there was no evidence that it had been occupied. As the section plunged, there was a sudden eruption of steam, bright flame, and smoke.

34. The first indication of anything unusual about the *Carl D. Bradley*, as noted by the *Cristian Sartori*, was about 1730 when the lights in the forward end were observed to go out. This was followed several minutes later by an explosion with considerable illumination and heavy smoke. When the smoke cleared, the *Carl D. Bradley* had disappeared from view and, whereas they had been getting a good image on the radar, there was now none. The *Cristian Sartori* changed course to 195 degrees true and headed toward the *Carl D. Bradley*'s position, and began a search for survivors, which lasted until relieved at 0200, 19 November. Searching proved negative.

Approximately one hour after the casualty, the *Cristian Sartori* sighted flares on the water about one mile off her port bow between the ship and Boulder Reef Buoy, and in line with the buoy.

35. The following Coast Guard units participated in the SAR emergency:

a. Plum Island Lifeboat Station – Heard "MAYDAY" at 1730 and dispatched CG-40300 at 1800. Due to heavy seas, this boat was unable to proceed and was recalled at 1900, arriving back at 2000.

b. Charlevoix Lifeboat Station – Heard "MAY DAY" at 1731 and dispatched CG-36392 at 1815. This small boat was recalled at 1855 on the recommendation of Commanding Officer, CGC *Sundew*, due to heavy weather.

c. Beaver Island Moorings – CG-36505 held in readiness and was not dispatched to the scene, due to the prevailing weather conditions and inexperience of the available personnel.

d. USCGC *Sundew* (WAGL 404) – Moored at Charlevoix, Michigan, in a twelve-hour standby status. The *Sundew* was alerted at 1740 by the Group Commander, Charlevoix Group. The *Sundew* got underway at 1820 and arrived in the search area at 2240. The Commanding Officer, CGC *Sundew*, took over operational control of the search, and coordinated efforts of all units from this time on.

e. CG Air Station – Traverse City, Michigan – This unit had one aircraft, UF 1272, returning from an air search in southern Lake Michigan and one aircraft, UF 2135, in a maintenance status. In addition, the station had two helicopters ready for flight; however, these were held in readiness, due to the prevailing weather conditions. UF 1273 was directed to proceed to the scene and arrived at 1915.

The ceiling in the search area was 2,000 feet, and this aircraft was used throughout the night in the search, and also to provide flare illumination for the surface vessels. A total of 88 flares were dropped during the night of 18-19 November. At daybreak, three HO3S helicopters joined in the search, and the UF 2135 was dispatched to Beaver Island to provide gasoline for the helicopters.

f. CGC *Hollyhock* (WAGL 220) – Moored at Sturgeon Bay, Wisconsin, in a 2-hour standby status. The *Hollyhock* was alerted at 1815 by Operations, Ninth Coast Guard District, Cleveland, Ohio, and was underway at 1830. The *Hollyhock* arrived on the scene at 0230 and reported to the *Sundew*.

36. The *S/S Robert C. Stanley*, anchored at Garden Island, heard the "MAY DAY", got underway at 1824, and proceeded to the search area, arriving at midnight. This vessel was joined by other lake vessels and numerous military and civilian aircraft as the weather moderated, and daylight on the 19th commenced. CG-40561, from Beaver Island moorings, and CG-40499, from Charlevoix Lifeboat Station, joined the search on 19 November.

37. Four crewmen, including Fleming and Mays, were able to board the life raft, which drifted rapidly away from the scene of the disaster. During the night, the other two were lost overboard as the raft flipped over several times in the heavy seas. The sea anchor also parted, leaving the raft completely at the mercy of the elements. On 0825 on 19 November, the *Sundew* sighted the raft with the two survivors, and Fleming and Mays were rescued at 0837 at a position 5 1/4 miles east northeast of Gull Island.

An overturned lifeboat was sighted at 0930 at a position four miles east of Gull Island. This boat was not occupied and was later recovered off the southeast tip of High Island on the 21st. During the day, 17 bodies were recovered by Coast Guard units in the area adjacent to and north of Gull Island. One body, that of Gary Strzelecki, one of the persons lost overboard from the raft during the night, was recovered by the merchant vessel *M/V Trans Ontario* at 1314 at a position close to the west shore of High Island. Each body recovered had an approved cork life jacket on, as did the two survivors.

38.   a. The following men survived: Total 2:

(1) Elmer Fleming, North Bradley Highway, Rogers City, Michigan
(2) Frank Mays, 925 Linden Street, Rogers City, Michigan

b. The bodies of the following persons have been recovered; cause of death – drowning: Total 18:

(1) Carl R. Bartell, 357 North First Street, Rogers City, Michigan
(2) Alfred Boehmer, 455 South 4th Street, Rogers City, Michigan
(3) Richard J. Book, International Hotel, Rogers City, Michigan
(4) Alva H. Budnick, Virgilene Trailer Court, Rogers City, Michigan
(5) William T. Elliott, Virgilene Trailer Court, Rogers City, Michigan
(6) Erhardt O. Felax, 685 South Lake Street, Rogers City, Michigan
(7) Cleland E. Gager, Onaway, Michigan
(8) Paul C. Heller, 1106 Riverview Street, Rogers City, Michigan
(9) Paul Horn, 448 North 4th Street, Rogers City, Michigan
(10) Raymond J. Kowalski, 1105 Dettloff Street, Rogers City, Michigan
(11) Joseph Krawczak, 645 South Second Street, Rogers City, Michigan
(12) Alfred Pilarski, 546 South Lake Street, Rogers City, Michigan
(13) Gary N. Price, Box 76, Onaway. Michigan
(14) Leo Promo, Jr., 419 St. Clair Street, Rogers City, Michigan
(15) Bernard Schefke, 506 South Lake Street, Rogers City, Michigan
(16) Gary Strzelecki, 234 West Michigan, Rogers City, Michigan
(17) Edward N. Vallee, 206 Superior Street, Rogers City, Michigan
(18) John Zoho, 853 Horton Avenue, Clairton, Pennsylvania

c. The following men are missing: Total: 15

(1) Douglas Bellmore, Onaway, Michigan
(2) Roland O. Bryan, Loudonville, New York
(3) John F. Fogelsonger, Medora Street, St. Ignace, Michigan
(4) Raymond G. Buehler, 1500 Cordova Avenue, Lakewood, Ohio
(5) Clyde M. Enos, 410 Ball Street, Cheboygan, Michigan
(6) John L. Bauers, 316 Hilltop Lane, Rogers City, Michigan
(7) Keith Schuler, 314 North First Street, Rogers City, Michigan
(8) Duane Berg, 372 North Third Street, Rogers City, Michigan
(9) Dennis Meredith, RFD, Posen, Michigan

(10) Floyd A. MacDougall,144 South First Street, Rogers City, Michigan

(11) Earl Tulgetske, Jr., 1912 Dettloff Street, Rogers City, Michigan

(12) Paul Greengtski, RFD, Posen, Michigan

(13) Melville Orr, 1113 Third Street, Rogers City, Michigan

(14) Dennis Joppich, 457 South Second Street, Rogers City, Michigan

(15) James L. Selke, 795 South First Street, Rogers City, Michigan

39. All the persons reported to have been on watch in the engine room are among those still missing. Of the 18 bodies recovered, eight were from the forward crew, and ten were from the after crew.

40. Radio Station WAD, Port Washington, assumed the radio control on Channel 51 (2182 kc) in the SAR emergency and broadcast an order for radio silence at 1740. This initial order was repeated a number of times by WAD and other stations in the mideastern and eastern United States. The imposed radio silence was lifted at 1840 on 19 November, and the active search was discontinued on 21 November 1958 by Office of the Commander, Ninth Coast Guard District, pending further developments.

Serious interference on channel 51 was reported. This interference was primarily from the unauthorized use of channel 51 by vessels on the Ohio and Mississippi Rivers, and partly from the failure of some Great Lakes area stations and vessels to maintain silence. The interference, however, was not serious enough to interfere with the on-the-scene communications among the vessels and planes actively engaged in the search.

41. Boulder Reef lighted bell buoy (LL 2163) was on station and showing its proper characteristics at 1410 on 19 November when checked by CGC *Sundew*.

42. In the vicinity of Boulder Reef, shoal water of 60 feet in depth or less extends over an area which is approximately six miles long and

three miles wide. The area circumscribed by this 60-foot depth curve runs mainly to the north northeast of Boulder Reef, which is marked on its southwest edge by Boulder Reef lighted buoy. The reef has a minimum depth of 15 feet adjacent to the buoy, and the shoal area of 30 feet or less extends to a distance of about 1 ½ miles northward from the buoy.

43. Aircraft from Coast Guard Air Station, Traverse City, spent a total of 122 hours searching the casualty area from 18 November to 9 December. During this time, no evidence of the sunken hulk or large wreckage therefrom was sighted by the aircraft. Miscellaneous small pieces of wreckage were found, both by aircraft and searching parties, on the west shores of High and Beaver Islands. On 20 November, Coast Guard aircraft UF 2135 sighted an oil slick, resulting from oil bubbling to the surface from an underwater source. The source of this oil slick, which was feathering out downwind, was located 5 ½ miles distant from Boulder Reef, on a bearing 314 true.

On 2 December 1958, the *Sundew*, sounding this area, noted on their depth recorder, type AN/UQN-IC, an irregularity in soundings which indicated a 25-foot pinnacle in 300 feet of water at the reported source of the oil slick. An immediate re-sounding of this area failed to again show the pinnacle, and later attempts to relocate it have likewise proven unsuccessful. Attempts to locate the hulks by soundings were made by the CGC *Mackinaw* (WAGB 83) and the *Sundew* during January and February; however, unfavorable weather conditions curtailed these efforts. Further attempts will be made when weather conditions improve.

44. The Board takes judicial notice of the following facts:

a. Records indicate that November is a month of severe storms on the Great Lakes. The storm of 17-19 November 1958 has been described by various ship masters as the most severe they have encountered. The publication "Shipwrecks of the Lakes", by Dana T. Bowen, reveals that between 1900 and 1950, over one-third of the vessels lost by foundering were lost during November, and over one-half of all strandings occurred in November.

b. The trade followed by the self-unloading-type vessels is extremely hard on the vessels. The self-unloaders load and discharge many more cargoes per year than do the conventional bulk freighters engaged in the iron ore trade. Likewise, these vessels frequent out of the way places in shallow water, and often ground and rub bottom while approaching docks. In addition, because of the short hauls between loading and unloading ports, the self-unloaders spend considerably more time at near maximum speed in the shallow rivers than do the conventional lake vessels.

c. The past inspection books, dry-dock examination books, and other official records of the Coast Guard were examined by the Board, and they revealed nothing of note concerning the *Carl D. Bradley*, except as mentioned elsewhere in the record concerning the last dry-docking in 1957 at Chicago, Illinois.

d. The official survey records of Lloyd's Register of Shipping were examined by the Board, and these records revealed nothing of note concerning the *Carl D. Bradley*. Extracts from the survey, in conjunction with the drydocking in 1957 at Chicago, Illinois, are included in the record.

e. Section 726 of Department of the Navy Publication NWP-37, Search and Rescue, indicates that the wind current would be up to 30 degrees to the right of the wind direction, in direction of 045 true to 075 true.

OPINIONS

1. That the *Carl D. Bradley* did not strike Boulder Reef, but that she broke in half in deep water in a position about five miles to the northwestward of Boulder Reef.

2. That the vessel could not have proceeded more than one mile between the time of the initial thud and the time she broke in half, and that the *Carl D. Bradley* continued on course during this period.

3. That had the vessel struck Boulder Reef, both parts of the hulk, by reason of their dimensions, would be visible in the water of less than 60-foot depth, which extends for a distance of about three miles northeast of the reef along the track the *Carl D. Bradley* would have made.

4. And further, that, having in mind the manner in which the vessel broke and the way the stern section plunged to the bottom, the *Carl D. Bradley* sank in water considerably deeper than 60 feet.

5. Supporting the opinion that the *Carl D. Bradley* did not strike Boulder Reef are the facts established relative to the navigation of both the *Carl D. Bradley* and the *M/V Cristian Sartori*.

6. That the cause of the casualty was due to the excessive hogging stresses imposed upon the vessel by reason of her placement in a ballasted condition upon the waves encountered at the particular instant of breaking. There were no facts disclosed by the testimony, or through the examination of the files on the *Carl D. Bradley* maintained by the U.S. Coast Guard, or Lloyd's Registry of Shipping, which would lead to an opinion that there existed any defects in the area where the break occurred.

However, it is felt that the appearance of hairline fractures in the vessel's bottom plating, as found in drydock, may be of significance in a technical study of this casualty by the Ships' Structure Committee, or other technical body, although the Board could find no indication of a relationship between this casualty and these earlier-noted hairline fractures.

7. That the eruption of steam, flames, and smoke, noticed by the survivors and the *Cristian Sartori*, occurred after the vessel parted,

and was caused by water rushing into the combustion chambers of the boilers as the stern section plunged. The fact that all bodies from the after end that were recovered were victims of drowning, with no indication of burns or violence, supports the conclusion that the reported explosion was actually the eruption of steam and combustible materials from the boiler out through the stack.

8. That the vessel was seaworthy at the time of her completion of her annual inspection at Calcite, Michigan, on 17 April 1958, and that there is no reason to conclude from the testimony or from reasonable interpretation of other known facts that she was not in such condition upon departure from Gary, Indiana, on 17 November 1958.

9. That the vessel was properly manned and equipped in accordance with existing regulations, and properly secured for sea upon departure from Gary, Indiana.

10. That the temporary repairs to the cargo hold, made in the winter of 1957-58, did not contribute to this casualty.

11. That the two unreported damages known to have been incurred during the 1958 season at Cedarville, Michigan, were minor in nature and of such location on the hull as to not have contributed to this casualty.

12. That the watertight door in bulkhead 173 at the forward end of the machinery spaces was not completely dogged at the time of the casualty, and that the watertight integrity of the vessel was thereby impaired. It appears likely that the door became undogged by some reason unknown and then swung open, allowing the free entry of water from the tunnel to the engine spaces.

It is felt that, had the door been completely dogged and thus maintained bulkhead 173 watertight, additional buoyancy would have been provided, and the speed with which the stern section sank would have been materially reduced.

13. That the drownings of those crewmen whose bodies were recovered were caused by the inhalation of the heavy spray. Because of the low water and air temperatures, and extremely rough seas, no type of life jacket could have enabled any person to have survived the 16-hour ordeal in the water.

Further, that the type of life jacket worn by the victims caused fatigue by reason of the need to exert constant arm pressure on the jacket to keep it down on the body while in the water. It is the opinion of the Board that the cork life preservers are not a satisfactory type for sustained support in the water because of the way they fit.

14. That the drift and set of the life raft, lifeboat, and bodies carried them north of Gull Island and to the eastward. This drift and set is in fair agreement with what might be expected from the information contained in Section 276 of NWP 37, Search and Rescue Manual, although it is realized that the application of the theories developed in this manual to the relatively shallow waters of the area in question might not be unqualifiedly accepted.

15. That efforts made by the crew in attempting to lower the starboard lifeboat were thwarted by the short time the stern section remained on an even keel. With the prevailing weather conditions and the quick settling of the after section, it is considered extremely doubtful that a launching of a lifeboat in the vicinity of the vessel's counter by use of the falls fitted with common hooks could have been successfully accomplished.

16. That the search and rescue operations in this casualty were thorough and well-directed. All Coast Guard units responded to the maximum of their ability under the existing weather conditions, and the major floating units were underway well within the time period allowed by their standby status.

The appreciation of the survivors and representatives of the owners of the *Carl D. Bradley* for the efforts of the CGC *Sundew* is worthy of note. The decision of the responsible personnel attached to the Coast Guard Air Station to hold the available helicopters for actual rescue work in view of the weather conditions was based on sound judgment.

17. That the participation of the *M/V Cristian Sartori* in the search was in keeping with the finest traditions of the sea. This vessel was immediately headed toward the scene of the casualty, and made every effort to assist under extremely adverse weather conditions. The fact that the searching of the *Sartori* proved unsuccessful does not detract from the valiant efforts of the Master and crew to aid the crew of the *Carl D. Bradley*.

  The voluntary participation by other merchant vessels, as well as private, commercial, and military aircraft, and by the individual citizens of the various islands, was also commendable.

18. That communications pursuant to this SAR emergency were adequate. All stations in the area maintained radio silence when so directed, and the interference on channel 51 that did occur did not impede communications on the scene.

19. That had the life raft been equipped with rocket or parachute-type distress signals, the survivors might have been located during the night.

20. That it is the stated policy of the owners of the *Carl D. Bradley* to give the masters complete responsibility for the safety of their vessels and, therefore, complete freedom to anchor or postpone departure, if unfavorable weather or other reasons dictate such action to be in the interests of safety.

  In view of this, it is the opinion of the board that the Master of the *Carl D. Bradley*, in making the decision to and in proceeding across northern Lake Michigan from Cana Island toward Lansing Shoal, exercised poor judgment. This decision was probably induced by a zealous desire to hold as closely to schedule as possible, and because of this, he gave less attention to the dangers of the existing weather than what might be expected of a prudent mariner.

21. That no aids to navigation or uncharted or incorrectly charted area or objects were involved in the casualty.

22. That no personnel of the Coast Guard or any other governmental agency contributed to the casualty.

23. That there is no evidence that any licensed or certificated personnel of the *Carl D. Bradley* committed any acts of incompetence, inattention to duty, negligence, or wilful (sic) violation of any law or regulation.

RECOMMENDATIONS

1. That all jacket-type life preservers be provided with a crotch strap to hold the jacket down on the body and with a collar to support the head out of the water. In this respect the specifications for life preservers under 46 CFR 160.002-005 (Subchapter Q, Specifications) will require modification.

2. That a second additional life raft or other approved buoyant apparatus be mandatory for all Great Lakes cargo vessels of 300 gross tons and over, and that 46 CFR 94.10-40 (a) and 46 CFR 94.15-10 (c) (3) (Subchapter I, Cargo and Miscellaneous Vessels) be modified to require two life rafts, and to specify that one of these rafts shall be in the forward part of the vessel and one in the after part of the vessel.

3. That each lifeboat on all Great Lakes cargo vessels of over 3000 gross tons be fitted with mechanical disengaging apparatus. To effect this recommendation, the provisions of 46 CFR 94.10-5 (a) (4) (1) should be modified to include Great Lakes vessels and to require that all existing common hook installations be replaced with mechanical disengaging apparatus at the earliest possible date.

　　　　Further, that the provisions of this recommendation be

extended to include Great Lakes tank and passenger vessels of over 3000 gross tons, and that the applicable sections of 46 CFR, Part 33 (Subchapter D, Tank Vessels), and 46 CFR, Part 75 (Subchapter H, Passenger Vessels), be so modified.

4. That each lifeboat on all Great Lakes cargo vessels be equipped with two painters as required for ocean and coastwise vessels, and that 46 CFR 94.20-10 (a) and 46 CFR 94.20-15 (z) be modified accordingly. Further, that the provisions of this recommendation be extended to include all Great Lakes tank and passenger vessels, and that the applicable sections of 46 CFR, Part 33 (Subchapter D, Tank Vessels), and 46 CFR, Part 75 (Subchapter H, Passenger Vessels), be so modified.

5. That each lifeboat and life raft on all Great Lakes cargo vessels be provided with a unit of at least six parachute-type flare distress signals and the means to project them. This recommendation will require modification of 46 CFR 94.20-10 (a), 46 CFR 94.20 (a), 46 CFR 94.20-15 (hh) and 46 CFR 94.20-25 (m).

Further, that the provisions of this recommendation be extended to include all Great Lakes tank and passenger vessels, and that the applicable sections of 46 CFR, Part 33 (Subchapter D. Tank Vessels) and 46 CFR, Part 75 (Subchapter H, Passenger Vessels), be so modified.

6. Inasmuch as the exact location of the hull of the *Carl D. Bradley* is unknown at this time, and the possibility exists that reasonable efforts to locate the hull during this coming shipping season will be successful, which may or not alter the findings of fact, opinions, or recommendations of this board, it is recommended that the board remain in an adjourned status so that it may be reconvened should circumstances demand.

JOSEPH A. KERRINS
Rear Admiral, U.S. Coast Guard
Chairman

JOSEPH CHANGE
Commander, U.S. Coast Guard
Member

CHARLES E. LEISING
Commander, U.S. Coast Guard
Member

GARTH M. READ
Lieutenant Commander, U.S.
Coast Guard, Member and
Recorder

UNITED STATES COAST GUARD

MVI
(CARL D. BRADLEY a-9 Bd)
7 July 1959

Commandant's Action

on

Marine Board of Investigation; foundering of the *Carl D. Bradley*,
Lake Michigan, 18 November 1958 with loss of life

1. The record of the Marine Board of Investigation convened to investigate subject casualty, together with its Findings of Fact, Opinions and Recommendations, has been reviewed.

Author's Note: Points 2-4 of U.S. Coast Guard Vice Admiral A. C. Richmond's action summarizes the Marine Board of Investigation's Findings of Fact concerning the Bradley's course from Gary, Indiana, to its sinking (Points 17-33).

REMARKS

1. Concurring with the board, it is considered that the *Bradley* did not strike Boulder Reef, but rather that she broke in two, and the eruption of steam and combustible materials as she went down gave rise to the mistaken assumption on the part of the *Cristian Sartori* witnesses that the vessel exploded.

2. Although in all probability the vessel broke in hogging, the implication in the Board's conclusion that the fracture resulted because the vessel encountered an unusual wave condition while in ballast is not supported in the record. In the absence of any evidence of improper or unusual ballasting, such reasoning would necessarily require an assumption that the waves were unique in the vessel's twenty-one year (sic) history of navigation in the Great Lakes.

This premise and the conclusion must therefore be rejected, particularly in view of the survivors' description of how smoothly the

-221-

vessel was riding; a point of which the Board took special note, and which was further reported by the statement of the Second Mate of the *S/S Johnstown*. For this reason the Board's conclusion that the Master of the *Bradley* exercised poor judgment in proceeding across northern Lake Michigan from Cana Island toward Lansing Shoal is also disapproved.

3. The Board has offered no other conclusions as to the possible cause of this disaster, and an extensive review of the record has likewise failed to yield any positive determinations in this regard. Contrary to the Board's opinions, however, the following factors may have had some causal connection, and cannot be discounted merely for the lack of probative evidence:

    a. The unexplained presence of the hairline cracks discovered in the vessel's underbody amidships during drydocking in Chicago in May 1957 strongly suggest the possibility of structural weakness.

    b. The two unreported groundings experienced by the *Bradley* in the spring of 1958 and November of 1958, may have introduced unusual hull stresses. It is because such possibilities exist that 46 CFR 136.05-1 requires a Notice of Marine Casualty to be filed with the Coast Guard in all cases of stranding or grounding, whether or not there is apparent damage.

    The possibilities raised by the foregoing, coupled with the fact that the vessel broke up and foundered under conditions which, while severe, she should easily have been able to weather, leads inevitably to the conclusion that the vessel had developed an undetected structural weakness or defect. Due to the significance of such a possibility, particularly with respect to other vessels of similar design and vintage, consideration will be given to the initiation of an underwater survey of the *Bradley*, depending, of course, on when and where the vessel is ultimately located, and any other practical aspects which might limit the benefits to be derived from such examination.

4. Regardless of any other determinations, this casualty has emphasized the need for the program of technical evaluation to determine if there is any evidence of structural defects in other vessels of the Great Lakes fleet. Such a program has been initiated. In addition, a reappraisal of present inspection procedures as applied to Great Lakes vessels is indicated, looking toward the adoption of such standards and methods that will increase the likelihood of early detection of possible structural defects, particularly in the case of older vessels.

The Commander, Ninth Coast Guard District, has been directed to make such a study with due regard for the peculiarities and problems attendant to the seasonal operation of Great Lakes vessels. In the course of such study, the Commander, Ninth Coast Guard District, has been directed to adopt any reasonable procedure within the framework of present laws and regulations, and to make further recommendations for any legislative or regulatory changes which appear necessary.

Finally, it is considered that this casualty has dictated a need for owners and operators to re-examine their responsibilities to establish and maintain safe operating and maintenance standards.

5. The Board's recommendations concerning life jacket crotch straps, an additional life raft, lifeboat mechanical disengaging apparatus, lifeboat painters and parachute-type distress signals merit further consideration, and will be made the subject of study by the Merchant Marine Council.

6. Subject to the forwarding remarks, the record of the Marine Board of Investigation is approved.

A.C. Richmond, Vice Admiral,
U.S. Coast Guard, Commandant

APPENDIX B

UNITED STATES COAST GUARD

5943/ SS CEDARVILLE
MV TOPDALSFJORD A-9
Bd 28 September 1965

From: Marine Board of Investigation
To: Commandant (MVI)

Subj: Collision between the *SS Cedarville*, ON 226492, and the Norwegian *MV Topdalsjord*, ON 36485, in the Straits of Mackinac, Michigan, 7 May 1965 with the resultant sinking of the SS *Cedarville* and loss of life

FINDINGS OF FACT

1. At approximately 0945R (EST) on 7 May 1965, the American *SS Cedarville* and the Norwegian *MV Topdalsfjord* collided in fog in the Straits of Mackinac, Michigan. As a result, the *SS Cedarville* sank at approximately 1025R on the same day with the loss of seven lives therein. In addition, there are three more crew members still missing. 16 other crew members of the *SS Cedarville* were injured, while nine were rescued uninjured.

The loss of the *Cedarville* was estimated at $3, 500, 000, with an additional cargo loss of $21,000. There were no injuries or loss of life on the *MV Topdalsfjord* and the damage, confined to the bow section, was estimated at $30,000.

2. The following are vessel particulars:

Name:	CEDARVILLE	TOPDALSFJORD
Official Number:	226492	36485
Service:	Freight (Self-Unloader)	Freight
Gross Tons:	8,575	5,839.81
Net Tons:	6,229	3,343.28
LOA:	603.9	423.6
Breadth:	60.2	54.0
Depth:	32.0	--
Propulsion:	Steam Reciprocating	Diesel
Horsepower:	2,200	6,200
Home Port:	New York, NY	Oslo, Norway
Built:	River Rouge, MI	Goteborg, Sweden
Year:	1927	1959
Owners:	US Steel Corporation New York, NY	Norwegian-American Lines, Oslo, Norway
Operators:	Lake Shipping-Bradley Fleet, Rogers City, MI	Same as Owner
Certificate of Inspection:	U.S. Coast Guard 28 March 1965	
Great Lakes Radio Certificate	FCC, 23 March 1965	QI–193 Canadian Govt 26 April 1965
Master:	Martin E. Joppich 146 South First Street Rogers City, Michigan	Rasmus Haaland Christophei Vei, #8 Oslo, Norway
License:	No. 246189	A-1461
Canadian Certificate of Qualification		#2307 (All Great Lakes)
Licensed Experience Great Lakes	19 Years	29 Years
Licensed Experience:	19 Years	19 Round Trips

3. Deceased crew members of the *Cedarville* are as follows:

Frank Donald Lamp, 578 W. Friedrich Street, Rogers City, Michigan. License No. 246197, BK-#209235, Chief Engineer. Next-of-kin, Mrs. Alice Marie Lamp, Wife, same address

Reinhold Frederick Radtke, 416 Brege Drive, Rogers City Michigan. License No. 261980, Z-955172 D-1, Third Assistant Engineer. Next-of-kin, Mrs. Rita Radtke, Wife, same address

Wilbert W. Bredow, 636 S. Second Street, Rogers City Michigan. BK-#140362, Steward. Next-of-kin, Mrs. Cecelia Bredow, wife, same address

Edward H. Jungman, Frederic, Michigan. Z-835668, Deckwatchman. Next-of-kin, Mrs. Jennie Lee Jungman, Wife, same address

Arthur J. Fuhrman, 764 N. Charles Street, Rogers City, Michigan. Z-1073496, Deckwatchman. Next-of-kin, Mrs. Barbara Fuhrman, Wife, same address

Stanley Haske, 425 S. First Street, Rogers City, Michigan. Z-80924 D-1, Wheelsman. Next-of-kin, Mrs. Elizabeth Haske, Wife, same address

William B. Asam, 324 N. Sixth Street, Rogers City, Michigan. Z-857730 D-1, Wheelsman. Next-of-kin, Mrs. Patricia Asam, Wife, same address

4. The crew members of the *Cedarville* who are missing as a result of this casualty are as follows:

Charles H. Cook, Route No. 1, Bradley Highway, Rogers

City, Michigan. License No. 246175, BK-#140598, Third Mate. Next-of-kin, Mrs. Jean Cook, Wife, same address

Eugene F. Jones, 451 S. Second Street, Rogers City, Michigan. BK-#072522, Stokerman. Next-of-kin, Mrs. Marion Jones, Wife, same address

Hugh Wingo, 439 N. State Street, Rogers City, Michigan. BK-#130807, Oiler. Next-of-kin, Mrs. Ila Wingo, Wife, same address

5. The crew members of the *Cedarville* who were reported injured as a result of the casualty and the subsequent exposure and immersion are as follows:

Martin E. Joppich, 146 S. First Street, Rogers City, Michigan, Master-BK#140534.

Leonard T. Gabrysiak, 336 E. Huron Avenue, Rogers City, Michigan, Wheelsman - Z-955875

Angus Domke, RFD #1, Box 72, Rogers City, Michigan, Watchman - BK-#252165

Ivan Trafelet, Millersburg, Michigan, Watchman, - Z-1073664 D-1

Edward Brewster, 441 W. Brege Drive, Rogers City, Michigan, Watchman - Z-955690

Robert G. Bingle, 305 S. Fourth Street, Rogers City, Michigan, Deckwatchman, Z-1140620

Larry D. Richard, 183 S. Second Street, Rogers City, Michigan, Deck Hand, Z-1185766

Elmer H. Emke, Posen, Michigan, Deck Hand, Z-1149624

Harry H. Bey, White Birch Lane, Rogers City, Michigan, Second Assistant Engineer - BK-#129864

Michael J. Idalski, 778 Charles Street, Rogers City, Michigan Third Assistant Engineer - BK-#094839

William J. Friedhoff, 1396 Spruce Street, Rogers City, Michigan, Oiler - Z-1097490

Billy R. Holley, 1175 D'Vincent Street, Rogers City, Michigan, Stokerman - Z-995143

Anthony Rosmys, Posen, Michigan, Stokerman - BK-#314709

James G. Lietzow, 1265 Birchwood Drive, Rogers City, Michigan, Repairman Helper - Z-1200594

Arthur Martin, 439 St. Clair Street, Rogers City, Michigan, Second Cook, Z-107345

David M. Erickson, 1039 Birch Street, Rogers City, Michigan, Porter - Z-1133065 D-1

6. The weather condition at the time and place of the casualty was dense fog, with visibility estimated at 300 - 600 feet. The winds were light from the southwest, the barometer 30.24, and the air temperature 41 degrees Fahrenheit. There were indications of electrical weather disturbances in the Straits of Mackinac area. The water temperature was estimated at 36 degrees F.

7. The *Cedarville* departed Calcite, Michigan, at 0501R on 7 May 1965, en route to Gary, Indiana, with 14,411 tons of open hearth limestone and a crew including the Master of 35. The draft of the

Cedarville was 22' 01" forward and 22'05" aft.

8. The *Cedarville* proceeded to the Straits of Mackinac under the supervision and navigation of the Master. The Master, in conjunction with the officers on watch, Chief Officer H. Piechan to 0800R, and Third Officer C. Cook thereafter, was utilizing the RCA (3 centimeter) radar and the radio direction finder to establish their position. The radar gave readings relative to the vessel's head and had five scales – 1 ½, 4, 8, 20 and 40 statute miles.

The vessel was equipped with a gyro compass that was also being used. The gyro compass had been checked on the range leaving Calcite, Michigan, and had indicated no error. The vessel was also equipped with the usual Great Lakes AM and FM radiotelephones, which were manned by the Master. All navigation, communication and operating equipment was in satisfactory working condition prior to the casualty.

9. On the morning of the casualty, the deck watch officers were noting some of the pertinent operating data in the Bridge Log Book, and were using Lake Survey Chart No. 6 (Straits of Mackinac) or No. 60 (Lake Huron - Straits of Mackinac). The vessel's engine room policy was to record engine speed orders in the Engine Bell Book and pertinent operating data in the Engine Log Book. Of the vessel's records, only the Bridge Log Book has been recovered to date.

At the time of the collision, Third Assistant Engineer R. Radtke was on watch in the engine room, L. Gabrysiak was helmsman, and I. Trafelet was on the port wing of the bridge as lookout. Communication between the lookout and bridge personnel was by direct word of mouth. The bridge wing was 25 feet aft of the stem of the vessel.

10. After clearing the harbor at Calcite, the *Cedarville* proceeded toward the Straits of Mackinac in light fog at full speed (88 RPMS - approximately 12.3 MPH.) Great Lakes fog signals were being sounded utilizing the automatic fog signal device. With Forty Mile

Point abeam at 0558R, two statute miles off, a new course of 305 degrees was set. Visibility was approximately one mile. The 305 degree course, which generally followed the indicated track line on the Lake Survey Chart No. 60, was continued to 0748R when the course was altered to 261 degrees gyro, using Poe Reef Light radio beacon (LL No. 1513 - 1965), and a radar range as a position fix.

At 0812R, with Poe Reef Light visible and abeam to starboard – approximately one mile off, the course was changed to 285 degrees gyro. At 0842R the Cheboygan Traffic Lighted Bell Buoy (LL No. 1524 - 1965) was abeam close aboard to port. Visibility, at this time, had decreased to one-half mile. No alterations of the engine speed orders had been given; however, the engine RPMS at 0759R and thereafter were noted in the Bridge Log Book as having decreased to 84 RPMS, caused by less deep water and not by personnel action. The average speed of the *Cedarville* from Forty Mile Point to Cheboygan Traffic Buoy was 11.7 statute miles per hour.

11. At Cheboygan Traffic Buoy, a course of 302 degrees true (302 degrees gyro) was set for the Mackinac Bridge Lighted Bell Buoy No. 1 (LL No. 1562 -1965). As on previous changes of course, the Master of the *Cedarville* transmitted a security call on Channel 16 (156.8 MC/S) and Channel 51 (2182 KC/S), announcing the new course and position of his vessel.

12. Approximately five minutes after assuming the new 302 degree gyro course, radiotelephone communications were established with the *SS Benson Ford*, downbound from Mackinac Bridge to Cheboygan Traffic Buoy. A passing arrangement was agreed upon verbally by both vessels, and one-blast passing signals were initially exchanged for a port-to-port passing, while the vessels were still two miles apart. The *Cedarville's* course was modified to 305 degrees gyro to facilitate the meeting situation.

The vessels passed each other without incident at a distance of one-half mile apart. The *Cedarville* did not see the *Benson Ford* visually. Although the Master of the *Cedarville* stated he had reduced his speed to half ahead (50 RPMS) at this time, there are no other records, testimony, or indications of any change in the engine speed orders to this point.

13. The *Cedarville* continued its 305 degree gyro course to keep clear of expected downbound vessels. Approximately three or four miles from the Mackinac Bridge, the *Cedarville* established radiotelephone communications on Channel 51 with the German vessel *Weissenburg*, which was approaching east in the Mackinac Bridge channel. When the *Weissenburg* indicated an intention to go down the South Channel, a port-to-port passing arrangement was agreed upon verbally by both vessels. The course of the *Cedarville* was altered to 310 degrees gyro to facilitate the meeting. Visibility was estimated to be 1200 feet at this time.

The *Cedarville* continued to sound fog signals. The lookout then reported underway fog signals from the relative direction of the Mackinac Bridge. They were also heard by the Master from his position in the front window in the pilothouse. Although the Master of the *Cedarville* stated he had reduced speed to slow ahead (25-30 RPM) upon communicating with the *Weissenburg*, there are no other records, testimony or indications of any engine speed order changes from full ahead to this point.

14. The *Weissenburg* passed under the Mackinac Bridge at 0938R, and about that time the German Master told the *Cedarville* that there was a Norwegian vessel ahead of the *Weissenburg*. The Master of the *Cedarville* attempted to communicate with the "Norwegian vessel" and arrange a passing agreement; however, no contact was made.

15. The Master of the *Cedarville* continued to get radar reports of a target - later identified as the *Topdalsjord* - from Third officer Cook on the radar. Under the Master's instructions, the range scale settings were alternately changed between the 1 ½, 4 and 8 mile scales. As the range decreased, two different versions of the events were related.

a. According to the Wheelsman, L. Gabrysiak, the course was steadied on 325 gyro, and the speed of the vessel was then reduced to half-speed ahead (50 rpms). The third mate then reported to the master that the other vessel was closing in on the *Cedarville*, and the bearing was not changing.

One-blast passing signals in accordance with the Great Lakes Rules were then sounded on the *Cedarville,* in between the fog signals, using the manual whistle controls. The last one-blast signal was a very long blast.

Shortly thereafter the *Topdalsfjord* was observed coming out of the fog at an estimated 100 feet. The engines were then placed on slow ahead (25-30 rpms). As the vessels converged, the master placed the engines on full ahead and ordered hard left.

b. According to the master, M. Joppich, the *Cedarville* was proceeding at slow ahead (25-30 rpms) on course 310 gyro with the third mate keeping him informed of the other vessel's bearing and range on the radar. Within the two-mile range no precise ranges or bearings were reported; however, the tendency of the other vessel to be "widening to port" was reported. One-blast passing signals in accordance with the Great Lakes Rules were then sounded on the *Cedarville*, in between the fog signals, using the manual controls.

After several unsuccessful attempts to make radio contact with the "Norwegian vessel" and with the range decreasing, the vessel's course was changed to the right gradually as recommended by the third mate. The *Topdalsfjord* was then noted looming out of the fog at an estimated nine hundred feet. The helm was ordered immediately hard right and full ahead was rung up on the engines. When the *Cedarville's* bow passed ahead of the *Topdalsfjord's* bow, the helm was ordered hard left in an effort to swing the stern clear.

16. The *Topdalsfjord* was on a steady heading and at right angles to the *Cedarville's* general approach. The *Topdalsfjord's* bow collided with the *Cedarville* at 0945R, abreast of No. 7 hatch on the portside at near perpendicular angle with only moderate impact felt. There

was no danger signal sounded on the *Cedarville* at or prior to the collision.

17. The *Topdalsfjord* departed Milwaukee, Wisconsin, at 1830R on 6 May 1965 en route to Fort William, Ontario, via the St. Mary's Falls Canal at Sault Ste. Marie, Michigan, with 1800 tons of general cargo. The draft of the *Topdalsfjord* was 14' 4" forward and 18' 6" aft. The bow on the vessel is ice strengthened and rakes forward.

18. The *Topdalsfjord* proceeded to the Straits of Mackinac from Milwaukee without incident. As the vessel approached the Mackinac Bridge, the Master assumed the supervision of the navigation of the vessel. The Master was assisted on the bridge after 0800 by the Chief officer, K. Fagerli, the Second Officer, J. Gronstol, on the radar, and the Radio Officer, A. Mellberg, on the AM and FM radiotelephones.
    The watch also consisted of wheelsman K. Oskarsen, and due to the estimated one-half mile visibility, a lookout, A. Bergkvist, was stationed on the bow. The bridge was approximately 200 feet from the bow.

19. The *Topdsalsford's* radar was being used for navigational purposes. The Decca radar gave readings relative to the vessel's head, and had range scales of 0.75, 1 ½, 3, 6, 12, 24 and 48 miles (nautical). The vessel was also equipped with a gyro compass, which had no error when last checked on the present Great Lakes trip. All navigation, communication and operating equipment was in satisfactory working condition on the day of the casualty.

20. After clearing Grays Reef Passage on 7 May 1965, the *Topdalsfjord* proceeded at full speed (average 118 RPMS) with stand-by on the engine telegraph, due to restricted visibility. Fog signals in accordance with the Great Lakes Rules were being sounded. At 0818R a radar position 094 degrees from White Shoal Lt., 3.1 statute miles off, was plotted. Inasmuch as the position was 0.7 miles north of the Lake Survey Chart 093 degrees track line from White Shoals

-233-

to the Mackinac Bridge, a new course to make 095 degrees good was set for the Mackinac Bridge. At 0850R the western edge of St. Helena Island was abeam with the intended course made good. An average speed of 17.4 statute miles per hour was attained between 0818 and 0850.

21. At 0903R the *Topdalsfjord's* speed was reduced to various maneuvering speed engine orders, including stop, as the vessel was navigated in respect to an unidentified vessel westbound from the Mackinac Bridge. The *Topdalsfjord* informed the German vessel *Weissenburg* following close behind her of the various speed changes being made up until the time of collision.

    Although security information was sent by radiotelephone from both meeting vessels, no mutual passing agreements were arranged, nor were sound passing signals exchanged. The vessels passed each other port-to-port at approximately 0927R, two miles west of the Mackinac Bridge without incident. The *Topdalsfjord* continued at reduced maneuvering speeds with visibility steadily decreasing. In the vicinity of the Mackinac Bridge, an additional bow lookout, Stale Gule, was posted.

22. At 0935R the *Topdalsfjord* passed under the Mackinac Bridge to the left of the center of the main span. The radar was operated then on the 1 ½ mile scale. The course was altered to 108 degrees gyro, as the Master then decided to take the South Channel route, instead of Round Island Passage, because of the restricted visibility. Two security calls denoting the position and new course were sent by Radio Officer Mellberg on the radiotelephone on Channel 16 and 51 with no reply. Shortly thereafter, a radar target 20 degrees relative on the starboard bow was reported at a range of 1.5 miles (nautical). Fog signals of a vessel underway were also heard in the same general direction.

    The fog signal of a vessel at anchor, later identified as the *J. E. Upson*, was also heard 60 degrees relative on the starboard bow, as well as that of the *Weissenburg* underway, astern of the

Topdalsfjord. In view of the relative position of the approaching vessel, the 108 degree gyro course was maintained on the *Topdalsfjord,* and the engines placed on dead slow ahead (approximately 40 RPMS 3-4 knots) at 0940R.

The radar bearings of the approaching vessel changed from 20 degrees to 29 degrees relative on the starboard bow as the range decreased to 0.5 mile as reported by the second mate. The engines were placed on slow ahead (50-55 RPMS, 6.5 knots) at 0942R. As the range continued to decrease, the second mate reported to the Master that the radar target was so large, accurate bearings or ranges could not be taken. The engines were then placed on stop at 0943R. The visibility at this time was estimated to be approximately 600 feet.

23. The Master of the *Topdalsfjord,* standing outside the wheelhouse door on the starboard side bridge wing, then heard one very long blast on a ship's steam whistle close at hand, broad on his starboard bow. As the whistle continued sounding, the *Cedarville* was then sighted by personnel from the bridge and bow, simultaneously looming out of the fog at a distance estimated to be 250 feet from the *Topdalsfjord's* bow. The *Topdalsfjord's* engines were placed on emergency full astern at 0945R by double rings on the engine room telegraph. 105-110 RPMS were attained on the engines in reverse prior to collision.

The helm was placed on hard right to augment stopping the vessel. The *Cedarville's* course was nearly perpendicular to the *Topdalsfjord's* course. The Cedarville's speed was estimated by the *Topdalsfjord's* bridge personnel at 6 to 8 MPH as it passed in front of the bow. The Master of the *Topdalsfjord* stated he noted his own prop wash advancing up the *Topdalsfjord's* side before impact.

At 0945R plus the *Topdalsfjord's* bow struck the *Cedarville* amidship at near right angles on the portside with only a moderate jolt felt. The *Topdalsfjord* was embedded in the *Cedarville* only briefly as the forward motion of the *Cedarville* swept the *Topdalsfjord's* bow around to a heading of approximately 037 degrees gyro.

The *Cedarville* continued on and disappeared in the fog. The engines on the *Topdalsfjord* were stopped at 0946R. There were no danger signals or passing signals sounded by the *Topdalsfjord* at or during events leading to the collision. The Master of the *Topdalsfjord* stated he was poised to sound a danger signal at the conclusion of the very long blast that was being heard, but since the *Cedarville* loomed out of the fog still sounding the long blast, Captain Haaland then considered a collision inevitable.

24. Following the collision, the *Topdalsfjord* drifted into the dense fog in the immediate area of the collision. The vessel's two lifeboats (one motor equipped) were prepared for launching.

   The boats were dispatched to search for survivors when the sinking of the *Cedarville* became known. The vessel drifted to 1115R, and then proceeded to anchorage near Mackinaw City. The lifeboats returned to the *Topdalsfjord* at about 1600R without having located any personnel from the *Cedarville*.

25. The approximate position of the collision was 078 degrees true, 6,600 feet from the south tower of the Mackinac Bridge. The average speed of the *Topdalsfjord* from the Mackinac Bridge to the collision was approximately 7 statute miles per hour. The full speed of the *Topdalsfjord* is about 17.5 statute miles per hour. The average speed of the *Cedarville* from Cheboygan Traffic Buoy to the collision was approximately 12.4 miles per hour. The full speed of the *Cedarville* fully loaded was approximately 12.4 miles per hour

26. There were no reported injuries to personnel of either vessel as a direct result of the collision impact.

27. No radar plot or computations were made prior to the collision by either vessel so that their respective target speeds, courses, or closest points of approach could be determined. The *Cedarville's* personnel did not record the engine speed changes or course alterations made prior to the collision in the Bridge Log Book.

28. The *Topdalsfjord* was damaged extensively at the bow section, extending back eleven feet. Flooding was confined to the forepeak area inasmuch as the collision bulkhead was not broached. The vessel was able to proceed on her voyage via Sault Ste. Marie, Michigan, to Port Arthur, Ontario, for repairs, and left the area of the collision at 1730 on 7 May 1965. The starboard bow plating of the *Topdalsfjord* was folded across the damaged bow to the portside.

29. The effect of the collision to the *Cedarville* was holing of the vessel at No. 7 hatch on the portside, above and below the water line. The damage was in the way of No. 4 portside and double bottom tank, in the vicinity of frame No. 100. Progressive flooding commenced immediately into No. 2 cargo hold, with only the stone cargo as a deterrent. The *Cedarville*, after impact, took an immediate list to port.

30. The collision and engine room W. T. bulkheads are located at frames Nos. 19 and 171 respectively. The area between the bulkheads, in addition to the three cargo holds, consists of the tunnel space, with the unloading conveyor system and seven side and double bottom ballast tanks on each side of the vessel. The ballast tanks were numbered from forward, No. 1 through No. 7, with the individual side and double bottom tank as a unit. Tanks Nos. 6 and 7 had trimming tanks that extended to the spar deck.

In the collision contact area, the top of the side tank was approximately three feet below the deep load water line. The bulkheads to the adjacent cargo holds and the hopper gates from the holds to the conveyor system in the tunnel space were not watertight. The design of the *Cedarville* is such that uncontrolled flooding in the cargo spaces will ultimately result in the vessel sinking.

31. Immediately following the collision, the *Cedarville* stopped her engines, sounded the general alarm, broadcast a MAYDAY message, and dropped the port anchor. Chief Officer Piechan went aft to assess the damage sustained in the collision. Captain Joppich radioed the

Weissenburg, asking for the name of the Norwegian vessel.

The collision was reported to the Mackinac Island Coast Guard Station at 0950R by radiotelephone. No tank soundings were taken. The chief mate reported by telephone later to the Master that the *Cedarville* was taking a tremendous amount of water in No. 2 hold over the cargo, and that an attempt to cover the hole with the emergency collision tarpaulin had been unsuccessful due to the size of the hole.

32. The *Cedarville's* two lifeboats, located port and starboard on the after house, were swung out and lowered to the spar deck bulwark. The crew, excluding those on watch and those assisting in the engine room, mustered in their life preservers on the spar deck and stood by awaiting further orders. The *Cedarville* was also equipped with a 15-person life raft forward, and a 25-person life raft aft, both of which would float free.

There was no panic, confusion or delay in preparing the lifeboats for use. The order to abandon ship was never given. Three life jackets were brought to the pilothouse, but only helmsman Gabrysiak had put his on before the capsizing.

33. As soon as the extent of the damage and its visible effects were realized, the Master of the *Cedarville* commenced operations to raise the anchor and to beach the vessel. At 1010R the Mackinac Island Coast Guard Station heard the *Cedarville* radio she was attempting to beach the vessel at Mackinaw City. The vessel came hard left, full speed ahead, taking the Mackinac Bridge Lighted Gong Buoy No. 2 (LL #1563 - 1965) close aboard to starboard. A course of 140 degrees gyro was set, as furnished by Third Mate Cook, to clear the *SS J. E. Upson*, anchored off Old Mackinac Point. However, the position of this anchored vessel was never accurately determined.

The Master transmitted several MAYDAY messages, and also instructed the *Weissenburg* to keep out of his way. At approximately 1025R the *Cedarville*, with little freeboard remaining, rolled over suddenly to starboard and sank, 120 degrees true, 17,000 feet from the south tower of the Mackinac Bridge. The distance traveled from the point of collision to where the vessel sank is approximately 2.3 miles. The distance remaining to the beach was approximately 2.0 miles. The *Cedarville* sank in an approximate heading of 140 degrees.

34. The distance from the point of collision to Graham Shoal was one mile west, and to Old Mackinac Point 2.2 miles. The course from the point of collision to the nearest land at Old Mackinac Point is 215 degrees T.

35. The *Cedarville* is presently lying deck down in 102 feet of water on her starboard rail, in two sections, broken at No. 7 hatch. The forward section is lying deck down about a 15-20 degree angle to the horizontal, and the after section is lying with its deck down at a 45 degree angle to the horizontal. The vessel and cargo have been surveyed and determined as unsalvageable.

36. The Chief Engineer F. Lamp and First Assistant Engineer W. Tulgetske went to the engine room after the collision. Inasmuch as there was (sic) no pumping orders from the bridge at this time, the first assistant went on deck and made a visual check of the collision damage, and returned to the engine room. Upon his return to the engine room, and based on his observations, pumping was commenced on No. 4 portside and bottom tank. The main ballast pump used was a recently installed 16" x 14" new electric pump, rated at 5,250 gallons per minute.

Each side and bottom ballast tank unit on the *Cedarville* was provided with one 8" ballast line located six feet above the vessel's bottom. Approximately four minutes after the pumping was commenced, telephone orders from the bridge to the chief engineer ordering ballasting of the starboard side. The electric pump was stopped, and the ballast manifold valves were adjusted to utilize the electric ballast pump to ballast one of the starboard tanks.

The task number is not known as the chief engineer, Lamp,

and oiler, H. Wingo, involved in the operation did not survive the casualty. After the electric pump commenced pumping into a starboard tank, a centrifugal steam pump, rated at 3,600 gallons per minute, resumed pumping out of No. 4 port tank. Two horizontal steam drag auxiliary ballast pumps, each rated at 2,000 gallons per minute, were then placed on the tunnel space sump well. The pumps being utilized all indicated they had suction and were operating properly.

Second Assistant Engineer H. Bey assisted in lining up the two auxiliary ballast pumps. The Nos. 3, 4 and 5 side and double bottom tanks each have a capacity of 1,042 short tons of fresh water, port and starboard sides inclusive.

37. With the pumps all in operation, the first assistant and second assistant left the engine room. The first assistant stopped briefly on the fantail and further tightened some leaking dogs on the gangway side port. Upon departing the engine room, he noted the inclinometer at 6" to port (1 degree). Shortly after arriving on the spar deck, the vessel heeled over to starboard suddenly and sank.

38. At some undetermined time but before capsizing, the Master telephoned the engine room to cease the ballasting operations, as the *Cedarville* had assumed an even keel.

39. As the *Cedarville* turned over to starboard, the crew standing by the lifeboats made last minute attempts to launch them. The No. 1 lifeboat was never released and sank with the *Cedarville*. The No. 2 lifeboat, with several crewmen aboard, was released from the falls as the *Cedarville* sank beneath it. Both life rafts floated free. The majority of the crew were thrown into the cold water.

40. Third Mate Charles Cook was last seen attempting to don a life preserver in the wheelhouse as the vessel heeled over. His body has not been recovered to date. Captain Joppich was rescued clinging to his life jacket. He had never put it on.

41. Eugene Jones, Stokerman, and Hugh Wingo, Oiler, were both on the 8-12 watch in the engine room and had been seen attending their duties just prior to the vessel's sinking. Their bodies have not been recovered to date.

42. The *Weissenburg*, under the command of Captain Werner May, made both lifeboats ready for immediate launching, and followed behind the *Cedarville* as she proceeded on course 140 degrees. At about 1030R the bow lookout of the *Weissenburg* reported hearing men crying out from the water ahead. At approximately 1033R the first man was seen swimming in the water. Shortly thereafter, both lifeboats were launched from the *Weissenburg*. Six survivors were taken from the water. The *Cedarville's* No. 2 lifeboat and after life raft with 21 survivors were found, and towed back to the *Weissenburg*. On board the *Weissenburg*, the survivors were wrapped in blankets and given stimulants.

43. Paul Jungman, Deckwatchman, one of the survivors, was dead from asphyxiation by drowning and shock when taken aboard the *Weissenburg*.

44. Stanley Haske, Wheelsman, one of the survivors, died on board the *Weissenburg* an hour later from shock and exposure.

45. At 0955R the CG-40527 departed Mackinac Island Coast Guard Station (five miles from the point of collision) in dense fog, and arrived on the scene at 1030R, joined later by the CG-36499. Immediate search operations were initiated; however, no survivors of the *Cedarville* crew were rescued by CG craft, as all survivors were picked up by the *Weissenburg*. At 1115R the CG-40527 found the forward life raft drifting and empty.

46. At 1042R the USCGC *Mackinaw* (WAGB-83) departed Cheboygan, Michigan, some 18 miles from the point of collision. Upon arriving in the vicinity at 1204R, it assumed command of the

search and rescue operation. At 1248R the *Mackinaw* moored alongside the *Weissenburg*, and took on board the survivors for transfer ashore at Mackinaw City, Michigan.

Search operations continued to 12 May 1965 with air craft from the Coast Guard Air Station, Traverse City, Michigan, USCGC *Naugatuck* (WYTM-92), USCGC *Sundew* (WLB-404), and units from Coast Guard Group, Charlevoix, also participating with negative results.

47. Commercial divers provided by US Steel Corporation from 10 May to 12 May recovered five bodies found trapped on the *Cedarville*. The bodies recovered were as follows:

> Donald Lamp, Chief Engineer
> Reinhold Radtke, Third Assistant Engineer
> Wilbert Bredow, Chief Steward
> William Asam, Wheelsman
> Arthur Fuhrman, Deckwatchman

CONCLUSIONS

1. The *S/S Cedarville* and *M/V Topdalsfjord* collided on nearly perpendicular headings in the Straits of Mackinac at approximately 0945 on 7 May 1965. The collision occurred with the *Topdalsfjord* on a course and heading of 108 degrees T.

2. The collision occurred in approximate position 078 degrees T., 6,600 feet from the south tower of the Mackinac Bridge in dense fog.

3. As a result of damage sustained in the collision, the *Cedarville* sank in 102 feet of water, 120 degrees T., 17,000 feet from the south tower of the Mackinac Bridge, at about 10:25 EST on the day of the collision. The vessel is resting on her starboard rail, deck down, in two sections, and is considered to be, with her cargo, a total

loss.

4. The three men listed as missing, namely Charles Cook, Third Mate; Eugene Jones, Stokerman; and Hugh Wingo, Oiler, are presumed dead as a result of the casualty. There has been no trace of them since the sinking.

5. The testimony of Helmsman Gabrysiak and Captain Joppich differs in several vital respects as to speeds and maneuvers before collision. The version as related by Gabrysiak is considered correct, and that as related by Captain Joppich is considered self-serving and false and is accordingly rejected. Hence it is concluded that the *Cedarville* was operated at full speed almost up to the jaws of collision.

6. There is evidence that the master of the *Cedarville* failed to navigate his vessel at a moderate speed in fog and restricted visibility, as required by Rule 15 of the Great Lakes Rules (33 USC 272). The speed averaged under reduced visibility, from the Cheboygan Traffic Buoy to the point of collision, coincided closely with the maximum speed potential of the *Cedarville* loaded. The *Cedarville* was allowed to proceed at full speed to the time of her evasive maneuvers taken in close proximity to the *Topdalsfjord*, ignoring the considerable momentum of the heavily-laden and comparatively low-powered vessel. The *Cedarville* had adequate advanced notice of vessel traffic approaching from the Mackinac Bridge from information provided by the radar, radiotelephone communications, and later the fog signals heard. A moderate speed under the circumstances would have provided more time to study the situation and react to the collision pattern that was developing.

The operation of the *Cedarville* just prior to the collision, relative to meeting and passing the *Benson Ford* at full speed after radiotelephone passing agreements, followed by the passing signals, would seem to indicate the intent of the *Cedarville* master to do likewise with the vessel traffic approaching from under the Mackinac Bridge.

7. There is evidence that the master of the *Cedarville* was timely informed, and aware of the sound signals of a vessel not more than four points from right ahead, and accordingly failed to reduce his vessel to bare steerageway, as required by Rule 15 of the Great Lakes Rules 933 USC 272) for vessels in fog or restricted visibility.

8. There is evidence that the Master of the *Cedarville* failed to sound the danger signal when there was no reply from the approaching *Topdalsfjord* to his one-blast passing signals, as required by Rule 26 of the Great Lakes Rules (33 USC 291). However as the *Topdalsfjord* already had initiated action to stop his vessel, this failure is not considered to have materially contributed to the collision.

9. There is evidence that the Master of the *Cedarville* was in doubt as to the intentions of the approaching Topdalsfjord and failed to reduce speed to bare steerageway, or as was necessary in this case, to stop and reverse when within one-half mile radar range of the other vessel, in violation of Rule 26 of the Great Lakes Rules (33 USC 291)

10. The *Topdalsfjord* was being navigated with reasonable caution under the circumstances and commensurate with the speed and power potential of the vessel. There were adequate bridge and lookout personnel assigned on the *Topdalsfjord* for its operation in restricted visibility. At the time of the collision, the *Topdalsfjord* was practically stopped.

11. In view of radar information available to the master of the *Topdalsfjord*, his decision to remain on course 108 degrees T., past the normal turning point for entry into the South Channel, is considered reasonable and consistent with the established principles of prudent navigation.

12. It is further concluded that no fault can be attached to either vessel for failure to maintain a radar plot, as the various speeds employed by the *Topdalsfjord* would have rendered a meaningful plot impossible.

13. The absence of a danger signal on the part of the *Topdalsfjord* prior to the collision is understandable under the circumstances in the case. The master of the *Topdalsfjord* first considered the approaching vessel to be passing him safely, as determined by the changing radar bearings. When the radar later indicated otherwise, the master of the *Topdalsfjord* was precluded from blowing the danger signal, although poised to do so, by the very long one-blast signal from the *Cedarville*. At the end of the long one-blast signal, the *Cedarville* was in view, and the collision was inevitable, hence a danger signal would have been meaningless.

14. The *Cedarville* sank as a direct result of the large ingress of water through the damaged portion of the hull sustained in the collision. Progressive flooding of the cargo holds and tunnel space could not be controlled due to the design of the vessel and the capability of the bilge and ballast systems. In view of the *Topdalsfjord's* forward draft and the rake of her bow, it is considered that the collision damage did not involve the *Cedarville's* ballast piping in No.4 side and bottom tank; consequently, there was no progressive flooding through the ballast system.

15. Since the vertical extent of the damage could not be determined, the action taken by the master to remove the port list by counter flooding is considered reasonable under the circumstances, as the ingress of water may possibly have been thereby lessened.

16. Since the master knew that, with the particular design of the vessel, any sizable hole into the cargo holds at deep draft would denote a sinking situation, his action taken of attempting to beach his vessel is considered proper. The master, however, judged poorly the

peril to his crew and vessel and the time remaining for him to beach his ship. He should have beached his vessel on the nearest shoal, or deciding against that, he should have steered the correct course for land. The beaching course furnished by the third mate was incorrect, and the master should have immediately realized this. It is tragic that the *Cedarville* steamed enough miles following her fatal wound to have made the beach at Mackinaw City.

17. There are no readily apparent or conclusive reasons why radiotelephone communications were not established between the *Cedarville* and *Topdalsfjord*. There are several reasons, however, that may have contributed to this.

a. The electrical disturbances present may have adversely affected Channel 51 at critical times of call.

b. The radio contact of the *Cedarville* and *Weissenburg* may have monopolized air time.

c. The late recognition on the part of the *Cedarville* master that a "Norwegian vessel" was ahead of the *Weissenburg,* coupled with the late awareness by the *Topdalsfjord* of the approach of the *Cedarville* as it appeared on the radar at only 1 ½-mile range, left little time for radio messages.

18. The Coast Guard units which were ordered to the scene of the collision responded in a timely manner; however, they were greatly hampered in their operations by the dense fog which covered the area.

19. The master and crew of the German *M/V Weissenburg* conducted rescue operations following the sinking of the *Cedarville* with dispatch and efficiency in the best traditions of the sea. It is considered that more *Cedarville* crew members would have perished

in the frigid waters had not the *Weissenburg* personnel performed so well.

20. There is evidence of considerable false optimism on the *Cedarville* that the vessel would be successful in its beaching operation. Due to this, a plan for minimizing personnel in the engine room was never initiated. The unexpected rapid heeling of the vessel to starboard precluded any final abandon ship order. The conduct of the *Cedarville* crewmen as they performed their assigned duties, notably in the engine room and in preparing the lifeboats, was commendable in that there was no confusion or panic.

RECOMMENDATIONS

1. It is recommended that further action under the Suspension and Revocation Proceedings of RS 4450, as amended, be initiated in the case of Captain Martin E. Joppich of the *SS Cedarville* concerning conclusions 6, 7, 8 and 9.

2. It is recommended that the Commandant recognize the gallant rescue operations of the German *MV Weissenburg* following the collision between the *Cedarville* and the *Topdalsfjord*.

3. It is further recommended that this case be closed.

W.A. BRUSO, CAPT. USCG, Chairman

T.W. POWERS, CDR, USCG, Member

A. W. GOVE, LCDR, USCG, Member and Recorder

Encl: (1) Transcripts of Proceedings
       (8 Vols, 30 Exhibits – 2 sets)
       (Fwd under separate cover)
       (2) CG-2692 - *SS Cedarville*
       (3) CG-2692 - *MV Topdalsfjord*
       (4) CG-924E - Frank D. Lamp
           & Death Certificate
       (5) CG-924E - Reinhold F. Radtke
           & Death Certificate
       (6) CG-924E - Wilbert Bredow
           & Death Certificate
       (7) CG-924E - Edward H. Jungman
           & Death Certificate
       (8) CG-924E - Arthur J. Fuhrman
           & Death Certificate
       (9) CG-924E - Stanley Haske
           & Death Certificate
       (10) CG-924E - William B. Asam
           & Death Certificate
       (11) CG-924E - Charles H. Cook
           & Death Certificate
       (12) CG-924E - Eugene F. Jones
           & Death Certificate
       (13) CG-924E - Hugh Wingo
           & Death Certificate
       (14) CG-924E - Martin E. Joppich
       (15) CG-924E - Leonard T. Gabrysiak
       (16) CG-924E - Angus Domke
       (17) CG-924E - Ivan Trafelet
       (18) CG-924E - Edward Brewster
       (19) CG-924E - Robert G. Bingle
       (20) CG-924E - Larry D. Richard
       (21) CG-924E - Elmer Emke
       (22) CG-924E - Harry H. Bey
       (23) CG-924E - Michael J. Idalski

(24) CG-924E - William Friedhoff
(25) CG-924E - Billy R. Holley
(26) CG-924E - Anthony Rosmys
(27) CG-924E - James G. Lietzow
(28) CG-924E - Arthur Martin
(29) CG-924E - David M. Erichson (sic)
(30) Statement - Angus Domke
(31) Statement - Robert Lucas
(32) Photographs (4)

TREASURY DEPARTMENT
UNITED STATES COAST GUARD

5943/ CEDARVILLE-TOPDALSFJORD
A-9 Bd
6 Feb 1967

Commandant's Action

on

The Marine Board of Investigation convened to investigate
the collision of the *SS Cedarville* and Norwegian
MV Topdalsfjord on 7 May 1965 in the Straits of
Mackinac with loss of life

The record of the Marine Board of Investigation convened to investigate subject casualty has been reviewed and the record, including the Findings of Fact, Conclusions and Recommendations, is approved subject to the following comments.

REMARKS

1. Concurring with the Board, it is concluded that the cause of the casualty was the failure of the Master of the *SS Cedarville* to navigate his vessel in a period of reduced visibility in compliance with the Statutory Rules of the Road. Despite the presence of radar, radiotelephone and recommended track lines, the primary anti-collision deterrent must continue to be in compliance with the Rules of the Road.

The prudent mariner must not allow habit, familiarity with route, frequency of passage or the presence of various navigational aids to lessen his duty to comply with the Rules of the Road.

2. Great lakes bulk carriers are not generally capable of withstanding unrestricted flooding of any main cargo space. When the collision occurred and the flooding could not be controlled, the vessel was in danger of eventual sinking.

3. In arriving at a determination as to the speed changes and maneuvers of the SS Cedarville prior to the collision, the Board accepted the testimony of the Wheelsman in lieu of that of the Master. Although the Third Mate who was also in the wheelhouse and the engineer on watch did not survive the casualty, this conclusion is supported by the record of testimony. It is recognized that in periods of crises the witness' recollection of facts is often at variance with the situation as subsequently determined to have existed. Accordingly, no further action concerning this conclusion will be taken.

4. During the final minutes prior to this casualty, Mr. Charles H. Cook, missing Third Mate of the SS Cedarville, was at the radar scope advising the Master. Records indicate that the license of Mr. Cook was endorsed as "radar observer."

5. Action concerning the evidence of violations of the Rules of the Road on the part of Captain Martin E. Joppich of the SS Cedarville has been taken under the Suspension and Revocation Committee.

6. The Secretary of Commerce, with the concurrence of the Secretary of the Treasury, has approved the award of a Gallant Ship Citation and Plaque to the German SS Weissenburg with ribbon bars to each member of the crew for their part in the rescue of the survivors.

W.J. Smith
Admiral, U.S. Coast Guard
Commandant

INDEX

Etched in eternal, gentle space,
A calming soul, nature's grace,
A rolling wave, that whispering sea,
Praise the new eternity
(JLH)

COLOPHON

Writing / Manuscript
Manuscript preparation: WordPerfect 10

Type
Body text : Times New Roman, 12 pt.
Chapter titles: Times New Roman Bold, 16 pt.
Quotations: Times New Roman Bold, 13 pt.
Captions: Palatino Linotype Bold, 11 pt.
Glossary: Palatino Lintotype, 11 pt.
Index: Palatino Linotype, 10 pt.

Pre-press
Cover Design: James L. Hopp
Proofreading: James L. Hopp / Mark Thompson

Conversion
Word Perfect 10 to PDF